Meer

Norbert Schneider

Johannes Vermeer

1632–1675

Veiled Emotions

TASCHEN

Contents

Vermeer of Delft

Vermeer's Life

We know very little about Vermeer's life. There is a tradition that he was baptised in Delft on 31 October 1632, the second child and only son of Reynier Jansz. Vos alias Vermeer. His father was born around 1591 in Antwerp. In 1611 he moved to Amsterdam where he specialised in the silk trade. He married Digna Baltens in 1615 and settled a short time later in Delft; at that time he bore the name "Vos", and from 1625 to 1629 he leased an inn, the sign of which was a fox, an allusion to his name. He continued to maintain his connections with the silk trade, although he gave art dealing as his main occupation upon being admitted to the Delft Guild of St. Luke in October 1631. This indicates that he followed a variety of trades simultaneously.

John Michael Montias has discovered that Vermeer's maternal grandfather, a watchmaker named Balthasar Claesz. Gerrits, was involved in some shady business deals. From 1619 onwards he and his accomplices used bought moulds to forge coins. This developed into an affair of such proportions that even the Public Prosecutor and Prince Maurit's governor became involved. Two of Gerrits's accomplices were condemned to death and beheaded. Gerrits himself managed to get away, to The Hague, and finally Gorinchem, where he seems to have lived on undisturbed.[1]

An entry in the Nieuwe Kerk registers shows that Vermeer's father bore the name "Vermeer" as early as 1625. In 1641 he bought the "Mechelen" inn, which lay in a good part of the town, on the northern side of the market square, for the sum of 2.700 guilders (not including the mortgage and high interest charges). The inn dated from the 16th century and, with a total of seven chimneys, offered luxurious accommodation. The patrons of Reynier's included members of Delft's refined and affluent bourgeoisie. These social contacts must have made quite an impression on Vermeer.

We know, from a document dated 1640, that Reynier had relations with artists such as Balthasar van der Ast (1593–1657; already famous in his own day for his paintings of flowers), Pieter Steenwijck (c. 1615–after 1656), and Pieter Anthonisz. van Groenewegen (1590/1600–1658). It may be that these gave the young Vermeer his first artistic leanings. Nothing is known about his training as a painter. All that we can say for certain is that he was admitted as a master to the Guild of St. Luke on 29 December 1653. This guild included painters in all

PAGE 6
Detail of *Woman in Blue Reading a Letter*
(ill. p. 52)

Because she was thought to be pregnant, the *Woman in Blue Reading a Letter* was formerly identified with Vermeer's wife; it is known that she bore fifteen children. However, attempts to work out the identity of this woman are superficial and do not contribute anything to our understanding of the meaning of this picture. The girl is wearing a farthingale which appears to be made of crinoline. This piece of clothing was highly fashionable at the time.

Rembrandt Harmensz. van Rijn
Rembrandt and Saskia in the Scene of the Prodigal Son in the Brothel, c. 1636
Oil on canvas, 161 x 131 cm (63½ x 51½ in.)
Dresden, Staatliche Kunstsammlungen, Gemäldegalerie Alte Meister

Carel Fabritius
Young Man in a Fur Cap (Self-Portrait), 1654
Oil on canvas, 70.5 x 61.5 cm (27¾ x 24¼ in.)
London, The National Gallery

Carel Fabritius, who had been a pupil of Rembrandt's in the 1640s and then settled in Delft in 1650, had extensive influence on Vermeer. Fabritius was killed in the explosion of the Delft magazine in 1654. An obituary describes Vermeer as Fabritius's successor: "The phoenix [Carel Fabritius] has departed from this world/ In the midst of life and fame/ A new master has arisen from the ashes/ Vermeer will follow in his steps."

genres, glass makers and dealers, faience makers, embroiderers and – art dealers, and until 1620 – carpet weavers too.

According to the statutes, a precondition for being admitted was a six-year apprenticeship to an artist recognised by the Guild. It has been suggested that this may have been Leonaert Bramer (1596–1674), but the stylistic differences between this artist (who went to Italy in 1614 and returned to his native town of Delft in 1624) and Vermeer are so great that there has been little support for the theory.

An alternative suggestion has been that Vermeer could have studied with Carel Fabritius (1622–1654; cf. ill. pp. 8 and 10), who was trained in Rembrandt's Amsterdam studio. Fabritius became a citizen of Delft in 1650, and joined the Guild of St. Luke in 1652. He was killed when the Delft magazine exploded, destroying much of the town. Dirck van Bleyswyck sang Vermeer's praises in a four-line piece in his *Beschrijvinge der Stadt Delft* (*Description of Delft*), calling him the "masterly" successor of the "phoenix" Fabritius. Although not too much emphasis should be placed on such an isolated comment, it nonetheless confirms that Vermeer was held in no little esteem in his own day.

Vermeer married Catharina Bolnes (c. 1631–1688) on 20 April 1653, in Schipluy, a small place near Delft. She was the daughter of Maria Thins (c. 1593–1680), who was at first opposed to the marriage. It may be, given that she herself was financially well off, and given that Vermeer's father was at the time in considerable debt, that she did not consider the marriage to be on a sufficiently secure financial footing. Another possibility is that there were problems at first because of their different religious backgrounds: Vermeer was a Calvinist, while Catharina Bolnes was Catholic. Leonaert Bramer was also a Catholic and put in a good word for Vermeer, and it was thanks to him that Maria Thins finally dropped her reservations. It has often been said that Vermeer caused Maria Thins to think more favourably of him by becoming a Catholic; however, there is no documentary evidence of this.

At first, the newly married couple lived in the "Mechelen," but then moved to his mother-in-law's house on the Oude Langendijk in what was known as the Papists' Quarter, near a Jesuit mission. Vermeer appears to have been relatively well off at this time, as he had no difficulties supporting his growing swarm of children. Catharina bore him fifteen children, though four of them died when still very young. He produced two paintings a year on average and he could scarcely have met these high costs of living from that income alone. There is no definite information as to whether he continued to work as the landlord of the "Mechelen," though such a second job was not at all unusual amongst seventeenth-century Dutch painters. We might mention Jan Steen (1626–1679), for instance, who leased the Delft brewery "de Slange" in 1654 (cf. ill. p. 9).

We can be quite certain, however, that Vermeer worked as an art dealer, like his father. He would have earned considerably more money by selling other artists' paintings than by selling his own. But he nonetheless continued to give his occupation as "painter" whenever he signed official documents. This tied in with his registration in the Guild of St. Luke; he twice held the office of Hooftman (syndic) on the Guild's ruling body, from 1662/63 and 1670/71.

Vermeer's relationship with Maria Thins had improved noticeably, as can be seen from the fact that his family moved in with her. Maria Thins was separated from her husband, Reynier Bolnes, the owner of a brickworks, but received a very large income from real estate, stocks and shares, and credit notes. She inherited several farms when her sister Cornelia died in 1661, and she leased out

Jan Steen
In the Tavern, 1660–79
Oil on canvas, 63 x 69.5 cm (24¾ x 27¼ in.)
Amsterdam, Rijksmuseum

Vermeer was admitted to the Delft Guild of St.
Luke in 1653. Besides painting, he also worked
as an art dealer. He presumably took over the
running of his father's inn, the "Mechelen," once
his father died. A contemporary Delft artist, Jan
Steen, who leased a brewery in 1654, painted a
number of scenes in inns. The situations he
paints cannot be relied upon to be completely
realistic however, as their intention is satirical.

one of them, the "Bon Repas" near Schoonhoven. The extent of Maria Thins's
wealth can be seen from a notarial inventory made in February 1676. It is an extensive list of the furniture, clothing and household goods contained in the elev-
en rooms, cellar and attic. Vermeer's family lived downstairs, and his studio,
with two easels and three palettes, was on the top floor. The studio contained the
heavy oak table which appears in many of Vermeer's paintings, together with the
equally familiar leather-covered chairs.

Maria Thins owned a series of paintings which Vermeer employed as *claves
interpretandi*, aids to the interpretation of his own paintings, and these included Dirck van Baburen's *The Procuress* (ill. p. 22 bottom), and a picture of *Christ
on the Cross*, which is probably the same as the painting that appears in the
background of Vermeer's *Allegory of Faith* (ill. p. 80). Vermeer also used items
of clothing, such as his wife's ermine-trimmed yellow satin jacket, in his paintings; he sometimes altered their colours, just as he also tended to adapt any
household objects included in his sets, adjusting their proportions to suit his
purpose.

Vermeer probably painted very little for the public art market, most of his
work being produced for those patrons who particularly valued his work. This
may also account for the modest number of paintings he produced. One patron
was the baker Hendrick van Buyten, who is probably the one whom the French
nobleman Balthasar de Monconys (1611–1655) visited when the latter stayed in
Delft in 1663. He made the following comment in his journal: "In Delft I saw the
painter Vermeer, who had none of his works to hand, but at a baker's we saw
one, in which there was only one figure, which had been sold for 600 *livres*, and
for which I myself would have thought six *pistoles* to be payment enough."
(A *pistole* was ten guilders.)

Vermeer's other patron was the Delft printer Jacob Abrahamsz. Dissius (1653–1695), who lived nearby on the Marktveld. Nineteen of Vermeer's paintings are mentioned in an inventory of his property dating from 1682. It is almost certain that the majority of the twenty-one paintings of Vermeer's auctioned by the art dealer Gerard Houet in 1696 in Amsterdam are these very paintings belonging to Dissius.

A clear indication of Vermeer's reputation as an art expert is that he was given what was then considered an honourable commission, to authenticate a collection of Venetian and Roman paintings which had been sold to Friedrich Wilhelm, the Elector of Brandenburg, by the art dealer Gerrit Uylenburgh (c. 1625–1679), for the sum of 30.000 guilders. He rejected the pictures as being "clumsy, slapdash copies." Vermeer journeyed to The Hague in 1672, together with fellow Delft artist Hans Jordaens IV (1616–1680), in order to contest the ascription of the paintings to Raphael and Michelangelo before a notary. He explained that they were worth at most a tenth of the sum Uylenburgh had asked.

Vermeer's later years were overshadowed by a dramatic deterioration of his personal financial position. He got into debt and had to take out loans. On 5 July 1675, he went to Amsterdam in order to take out a loan of 1,000 guilders. War had broken out between the Netherlands and France in 1672, with French troops advancing rapidly right into the northern part of the United Provinces, and this had had a ruinous effect on Vermeer. Dykes were opened as a last form of defence against the French army, and this flooded enormous tracts of land, including the land that Maria Thins had leased out at Schoonhoven. As a consequence, Vermeer was no longer paid the rent which had, till then, been a regular source of income for his family. That disastrous year became known as the "rampjaar," and from then onwards Vermeer did not manage to sell any more pictures. His wife later commented on this when talking about the destructive war with France: "As a result and owing to the very great burden of his children, having no means of his own, he had lapsed into such decay and decadence, which he had so taken to heart, as if he had fallen into a frenzy, and, in a day or a day and a half, had gone from being healthy to being dead."

Vermeer was buried on 15 December 1675, in the family grave at the Oude Kerk, Delft. He was survived by eleven young children, of whom about eight still lived at home. Catharina Bolnes now found herself hardly able to satisfy her creditors, and therefore felt it necessary to apply for the High Court in The Hague to take charge of the management of her properties. She relinquished all her rights of inheritance, ceding them to her creditors. Antoni van Leeuwenhoek (1632–1723; ill. p. 77) was appointed trustee of the properties. His main occupation was as a cloth merchant in Delft, and he was already internationally renowned for his inventions and discoveries in microscopy; he was made a member of the Royal Society in London in 1680.

At this time, the only paintings of Vermeer's which Catharina Bolnes still possessed were the picture known as *Schilderconst* (*The Art of Painting*, ill. p. 85), and the *Woman with a Pearl Necklace* (ill. p. 59). She gave *The Art of Painting* away on 24 February 1676, to discharge her mother's debts. Most of the other paintings were owned at that time by the printer Jacob Dissius, who died in October 1695. Several months after his death, twenty-one Vermeers were put up for auction in Amsterdam.

The 1696 auction catalogue, which included pictures by other artists (a total of 134 pictures were auctioned), is extremely useful, for it shows us that Vermeer

Register of the Delft Guild of St. Luke,
c. 1675
The Hague, Koninklijke Bibliotheek,
75 C 6 II, fol. 2v

The register of the Guild of St. Luke is one of the few documents to contain any information about Vermeer's life. Vermeer's name is entry 78, and Carel Fabritius, who was believed to have been his teacher, is entry 75.

was held in high esteem. It is striking that the estimates for his paintings are by no means low when compared to usual prices. For example, number 1 was the *Woman with a Balance* (ill. p. 61), which is now in Washington, D.C.; it was estimated at 150 guilders ("it is painted with great skill and vividness"). The price set at auction for number 31, the *View of Delft* (ill. pp. 16/17), was particularly high at 200 guilders. Compare this with Jan Steen, who once received that amount for three portraits, or Isaak van Ostade, who in 1641 sold thirteen paintings to an art dealer for 27 guilders. During his best period, Vermeer was clearly at the top of the price structure of the Delft art market; it is even said that, in or shortly before 1663, he was paid 600 guilders for a painting containing just one figure.

Detail of *View of Delft* (ill. pp. 16/17)

The buildings in the foreground, such as the Schiedam Gate are in shadow, while in the background buildings such as the Nieuwe Kerk's tall tower gleam brightly.

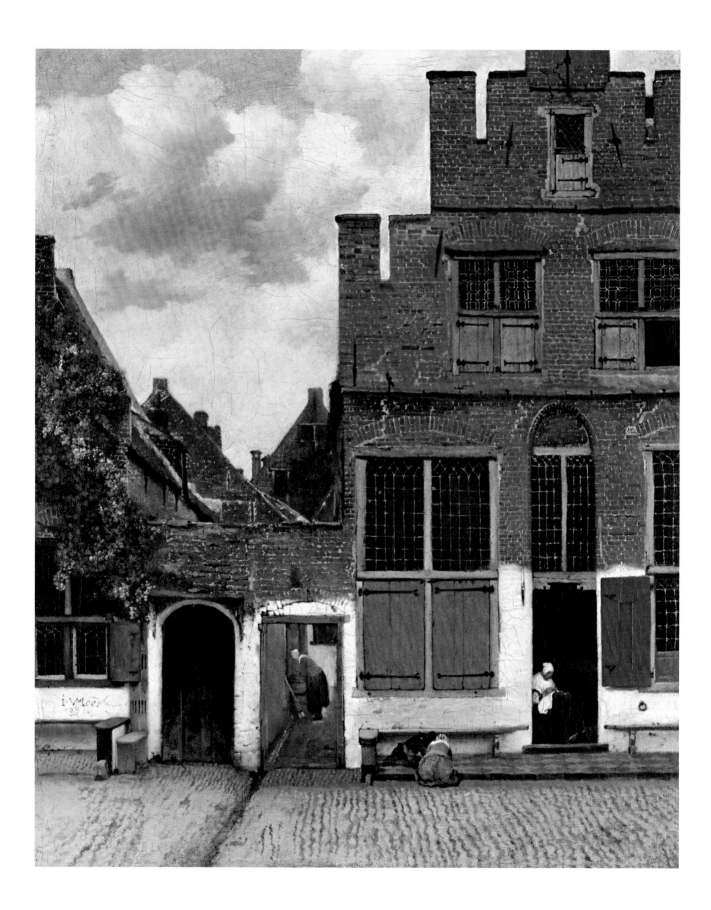

Views of Delft

The City and the Streets

Vermeer twice painted aspects of his home town of Delft. One such painting, kept in the Rijksmuseum in Amsterdam, is the small picture generally known as *Het Straatje* (*The Little Street*, ill. p. 12); the other is the considerably larger *View of Delft* (ill. pp. 16/17), in the Mauritshuis, The Hague.

Views of towns were not often painted for general sale in Holland, most of these pictures being official or private commissions. The prices that they fetched frequently greatly exceeded those paid for uncommissioned landscapes. In 1651, for instance, Jan van Goyen received the sum of 650 guilders from the city elders for his view of The Hague. The average price for ordinary landscapes has been shown in research carried out by J. M. Montias to have been about 16.6 guilders.[2] The auction catalogue of the pictures sold after Vermeer's death, on 16 May 1696, includes number 32, a view of Delft estimated at 200 guilders; this is a comparatively high price. It has been assumed that Vermeer planned his *View of Delft* using a camera obscura (ill. p. 16).

Willem Blaeu's 1649 Atlas, which contains town plans of Delft, has been used to identify the precise point, the upper storey of a house, from which Vermeer painted this picture. A relatively high viewpoint can be inferred from the angle at which we look down at the group of people on the banks of the Schie. The gentle diagonal of the river bank in the foreground is a compositional feature that can also be seen in Esaias van de Velde's (1587–1630) *View of the Zierikzee* (1618). It was Pieter Bruegel the Elder (1525–1569) who first introduced this triangular piece of shoreline into Dutch landscape art.

Taken as a whole, however, Vermeer remains faithful even here to the basic principle that informs his interiors, that of strong linear structures. Vermeer also attempted to give his painting a unifying colour scheme. Ochres and browns predominate, occasionally highlighted by red and yellow accents, such as the slate roofs that, depending on the positions of the clouds, are partly lit by the sun. Jacob van Ruisdael (1628–1682) aimed at similar light effects in the middle distance. In Vermeer's picture, the closer parts of the fortifications, such as the Schiedam Gate, are in deeper shadow, whereas the more distant buildings in the centre, including the soaring tower of the Brabant Late Gothic Nieuwe Kerk, gleam with an almost unreal brightness. It is safe to assume that Vermeer was making a deliberate political point by doing this, because the Nieuwe Kerk had,

Pieter de Hooch
The Courtyard of a House in Delft, 1658
Oil on canvas, 73.5 x 60 (29 x 23½ in.)
London, The National Gallery

Pieter de Hooch worked in Delft for a time, and was also a painter of domestic scenes. It is likely that Vermeer was familiar with his paintings.

PAGE 12
The Little Street, c. 1658–61
Oil on canvas, 53.5 x 43.5 cm (21 x 17¼ in.)
Amsterdam, Rijksmuseum

The façade of the house runs parallel to the frame in this painting. Vermeer paid special attention to the signs of ageing on the coarsely whitewashed brick façade. Though the overall impression is one of silent immobility, there is plenty of movement in the clouds passing overhead.

Pieter de Hooch
A Backyard in Delft, c. 1658–60
Oil on canvas, 69.5 x 60 cm (27¼ x 23½ in.)
Washington, D.C., National Gallery of Art,
Andrew Mellon Collection, 1937

Comparable to Vermeer's painting *The Little Street* are the pictures of back yards in Delft and of their inhabitants produced by Pieter de Hooch just before 1660 (ill. p. 13 and above). These scenes are, however, generally viewed from relatively close quarters, while Vermeer depicts his town houses from a greater distance.

PAGE 15
Detail of **The Little Street** (ill. p. 12)

Earlier Dutch artists, such as Pieter Bruegel the Elder, were very precise in their depiction of children at play, which for them had a moral purpose; in contrast, on Vermeer's painting, we are left in doubt as to what exactly the children are doing.

since 1622, housed the monument, made by Hendrick de Keyser, to William of Orange. William had been assassinated in the Prinsenhof in Delft in 1584, and was held in great respect by the citizens of Delft for his heroic role in the resistance to Spanish rule.

The dark buildings near the banks of the river are studded with tiny, granular dots of colour that make the cracks in the brick walls and the hulls of the ships such as the one near the crane on the right positively shimmer, breaking up their dark bulk. This aesthetic aspect of the picture is directly linked to the image seen through the camera obscura which Vermeer was using. So his topographical view of Delft can even, to a certain degree, be termed abstract, as the optical phenomena associated with this instrument – such as particular types of reflections and refractions and a lack of focus – are reproduced here at several points.

Vermeer was just as interested as Jacob van Ruisdael in the ever-changing clouds, which constantly altered the light falling on his subjects; and time plays an important role in this picture, too. The overall impression, paradoxically, is of calm and a lack of activity, however; this is undoubtedly linked to the nearde-serted appearance of the place.

The Little Street (ill. p. 12), which was probably painted at a somewhat earlier date, also conveys the impression of a timeless, silent lack of motion. We see, directly parallel to us on the other side of the road and beyond the rows of cobble-stones, a brick façade with deep-cut, embrasure-like gables, which are lower on the left, forming a link to the neighbouring house. The gables and roofs of buildings further away can be seen over the connecting wall. Most of the house's shutters are closed, which almost gives the impression that the house is sealed off from the outside world. Our only view of the interior is through the open front door, where we can see a woman busy lace-making; beyond her, all is dark. The gateway to the yard has been repaired in a rather rough and ready fashion, and through it we can see a narrow passageway where a maid is busy at a water butt or something similar. This is a motif that was to gain prominence in the work of Jean-Baptiste Siméon Chardin.

The two women, who are completely involved in their housework tasks, are anonymous. The maid is partly turned away, so that we cannot make out her face, while the features of the seated woman are little more than a blob of paint framed by the white of her bonnet, upper garment and pillow lace; this colour is continued through the coarse whitewash of the lower part of the façade. It is not possible to make out the faces of the two children kneeling on the ground in front of the house. It is also not clear what they are doing. They are probably engaged in the same sort of activity as the children one sees in Dutch seventeenth-century church interiors, helping to dig tiles out of the floor.

There is no communication between the few people in Vermeer's *Little Street*. Their quiet activities are all separate and independent of each other; nonetheless, we are invited to notice the parallel, simultaneous nature of these activities. The effect is similar in the somewhat earlier 1658 painting by Pieter de Hooch (1629–1684) called *The Courtyard of a House in Delft* (ill. p. 13). Vermeer was probably familiar with this painting. On the left, the lady of the house can be seen in the hallway that leads onto the street; on the right, quite separately, her young daughter is stepping out of a shed with the maid.

View of Delft, c. 1660–63
Oil on canvas, 96.5 x 115.7 cm (38 x 45½ in.)
The Hague, Koninklijk Kabinet
van Schilderijen Mauritshuis

It is thought that this view of Delft was painted
from the upper storey of a house. Contrary to
the practice of veduta painters, who were interested in topography and would have painted
the town in its entirety, he painted only a small
section. It is safe to assume that Vermeer was
making a deliberate political point in the way
he painted sunlight breaking through the dark
clouds and striking the buildings in the background. The Nieuwe Kerk is brightly lit; since
shortly after the turn of the century it had
housed the tomb of William I of Orange, a
monument steeped in national symbolism.

Athanasius Kircher
Camera obscura
in *Ars magna lucis et umbrae*,
Rome, 1646, plate 28

The general principle of the camera obscura had
been known since classical times, but it was not
used until the sixteenth century, and then mainly for topographical reasons. A portable version
was quickly developed, which projected the
image onto a piece of paper or glass plate, from
which the image could be copied onto another
medium. Vermeer probably used such an instrument while painting his *View of Delft*.

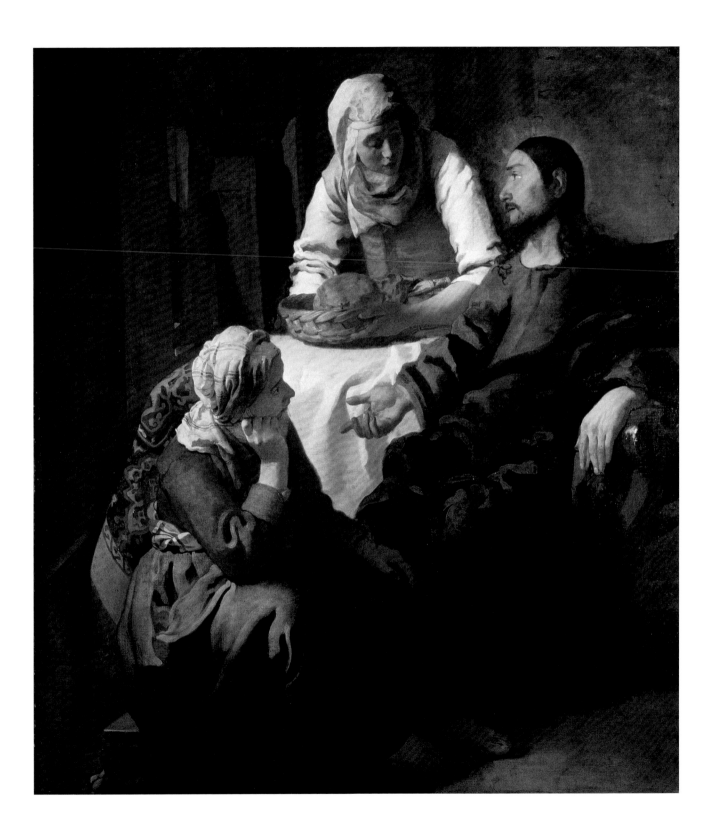

"Mary Has Chosen the Good Portion"

History Painting: a Most Distinguished Task

Given the many genre paintings done by Vermeer, it is perhaps surprising to realise that the earliest of his works known to us are of the type of paintings known in his time as histories. It apparently seemed important to the young artist (or it was expected of him) to prove that he possessed the abilities of a *pictor doctus*, an "educated artist," upon his admission to the painters' guild; such an artist would be able to inform what the art world considered to be lofty subjects with decorum, in a proper and becoming manner.

The Paris College of Art set the standards, and had developed a hierarchical structure of genres; history paintings occupied the top position – above portraits, landscapes, still lifes and animal paintings. Dutch art critics such as Karel van Mander (1548–1606) with his *Schilder-boeck* (Haarlem 1604, folio 281a) stated from quite early on in their treatises that history paintings were the most distinguished tasks in art. On the one hand, this genre included religious subjects, biblical motifs (cf. ill. p. 19) or scenes from the saints' lives and church history; on the other, it also included ancient historical subjects and mythological themes.

In contrast to many works of Vermeer's late period (such as *The Lacemaker*, c. 1669/70, 23.9 x 20.5 cm and thus Vermeer's smallest painting; ill. p. 4), *Christ in the House of Mary and Martha* is a relatively large painting (ill. p. 18). It depicts a New Testament scene from the Gospel of St. Luke, where the evangelist tells us how Christ went to a market, and was invited home for a meal by a woman called Martha. While Martha was busy in the kitchen, her sister Mary listened to Christ. Martha asked Christ why he did not ask Mary to help her serve, but he answered, "Martha, Martha, you are anxious and troubled about many things; one thing is needful. Mary has chosen the good portion, which shall not be taken away from her."

This section was already extremely popular in sixteenth-century Flemish art. It allowed people to deal with the problem of good deeds, which had been rejected by the Reformers as being superficial. At the same time, it was possible to demonstrate the humanists' favourite contrast, namely that of the *vita activa* (busy, active life) as opposed to the *vita contemplativa* (contemplative life).

Vermeer's *Christ in the House of Mary and Martha* uses a triangular composition that is comparatively straightforward and uncomplicated. The setting is a

Erasmus Quellinus II
Christ in the House of Mary and Martha,
c. 1640–1645
Oil on canvas, 172 x 243 cm (67¾ x 95¾ in.)
Valenciennes, Musée des Beaux-Arts

This work has repeatedly been identified as the probable model for Christ's pose in Vermeer's picture with the same title.

PAGE 18
Christ in the House of Mary and Martha,
c. 1655
Oil on canvas, 160 x 142 cm (63 x 56 in.)
Edinburgh, National Galleries of Scotland

This was one of Vermeer's earliest paintings. Paintings of biblical themes were classified as histories, which were described in treatises on art as most distinguished tasks. Vermeer probably wanted to demonstrate his abilities in this genre upon entry to the Guild of St. Luke.

Jacob van Loo
Diana and Her Companions, 1648
Oil on canvas, 136.8 x 170.6 cm (54 x 67¼ in.)
Berlin, Staatliche Museen zu Berlin,
Gemäldegalerie

PAGE 21
Diana and Her Companions, c. 1654
Oil on canvas, 97.8 x 104.6 cm (38½ x 41¼ in.)
The Hague, Koninklijk Kabinet
van Schilderijen Mauritshuis

Rembrandt Harmensz. van Rijn
Bathsheba with the Letter of King David, 1654
Oil on canvas, 142 x 142 cm (56 x 56 in.)
Paris, Musée du Louvre

An analogy of Vermeer's scene of Diana's feet
being washed (ill. p. 21) is this picture by Rembrandt, which was painted at about the same
time. This motif produced a typological relation
between Diana and Bathsheba, and Christ.

simple room with wooden walls. Mary is sitting at the front, on a low stool, at
the feet of Christ; his head is surrounded by a weak halo, and he is seated on an
armchair with voluted arms. Martha is bringing in a basket of bread, and he is
showing her, by pointing his outstretched hand at Mary, that the latter has chosen the better portion. Mary has taken off her shoes; this is a sign of humility.
Her posture – or, to be precise, the way she is supporting her head on her hand –
is in accordance with the iconography of melancholy. Here it stands for pensive-
ness and spiritual contemplation, in the sense of the *vita contemplativa*.

Vermeer applied the colours pastose with a wide brush. This can be seen
particularly clearly at the folds in the garments, which are raised roughly. He
favoured strong, intense colour contrasts, such as the dazzling white of the
tablecloth, strikingly contrasted with Christ's dark blue robe and Mary's vermilion blouse.

Vermeer's second history painting from his early period is *Diana and Her
Companions*, now in the Mauritshuis, The Hague (ill. p. 21). The theme is borrowed from Ovid's *Metamorphoses* (3, 138–253). In Roman mythology, Diana was
the goddess of hunting, and she was considered to be the embodiment of chastity. The motif of the bathing goddess was a particularly good way of demonstrating this aspect of virgin purity, strict morality and the sense of shame, which is
being offended by the voyeurism of the approaching Actaeon. In 1556–59, Titian
(c. 1490–1576) painted this later scene – which, according to Ovid, takes place
immediately after the episode depicted by Vermeer – for King Philip II of Spain
(*Diana and Actaeon*, London, National Gallery). His subject was nudity, which
was at that time beginning to be considered an embarrassing subject.
Paradoxically, the artist's liberal portrayal invites voyeurism on the part of his
audience, but this is inherently condemned within the picture. In contrast to
Titian's erotic and sensual interpretation of the subject, Vermeer's painting seems
to lack action and is positively prudish. This tendency to conceal nudity, which
was considered to be offensive, can also be seen in the earlier 1648 painting by
another Dutchman, the Amsterdam artist Jacob van Loo (1614–1670). It is possible that this painting was one of Vermeer's sources (ill. p. 20 top). In Vermeer's
painting, a partially clad nymph (behind Diana, who can be recognised by her
crescent-shaped diadem) is turning away modestly.

Vermeer depicted only a small number of people in this picture. Diana and
two of her companions are sitting on a stone, resting after the hunt. In the background is a darkly-clad nymph, who is reverently, even somewhat apathetically,
watching the ritual action that another nymph is carrying out, that of washing
the goddess's feet. This motif is used by Vermeer to create a typological connection between Diana and Christ, which gives the painting an almost religious
dimension. There is another parallel to this in the washing of Bathsheba's feet
(2 Samuel, 11; ill. p. 20 bottom), which was painted at almost exactly the same
point in time by Rembrandt (1606–1669).

Dusk is beginning to fall, and a heavy, melancholy mood is weighing on this
evening scene. The faces of the women are in shadow. This darkness can be associated with the fact that, in classical mythology, Diana was often equated with
the moon goddess, Selene (hence the crescent diadem). She was also considered
to help with births, as the moistness of the moon was thought to aid delivery.

This early painting still has many faults and weaknesses, in particular where
the depiction of the positions and movements of the bodies are concerned.
There is no overlooking the qualitative difference between this and Jacob van
Loo's painting, the latter being much more elegant in terms of its composition

Frans van Mieris the Elder
The Soldier and the Prostitute, 1658
Oil on board, 42.8 x 33.3 cm (17 x 13 in.)
The Hague, Koninklijk Kabinet
van Schilderijen Mauritshuis

PAGE 23
The Procuress, 1656
Oil on canvas, 143 x 130 cm (56¼ x 51¼ in.)
Dresden, Staatliche Kunstsammlungen,
Gemäldegalerie Alte Meister

Dirck van Baburen
The Procuress, 1622
Oil on canvas, 101 x 107 cm (39¾ x 42¼ in.)
Boston, Museum of Fine Arts,
M. Theresa B. Hopkins Fund

This painting by Baburen, which is set in a
house of ill repute, belonged to Vermeer's
mother-in-law. It appears, as a painting within
a painting, in two of Vermeer's paintings, and
was, in addition, probably the stimulus for his
own painting of the same name.

and execution. Measured against high academic standards, Vermeer's composition makes a clumsy and provincial impression. There have long been doubts
as to whether this is really one of Vermeer's works, doubts that cannot be completely dispelled. For instance, the painting was ascribed to Nicolaes Maes
(1634–1693), who was trained in Rembrandt's studio, when it was bought by
the Mauritshuis in 1876. In addition, John Nash has noticed a "distinctly
Rembrandtian air"[3] about the painting.

Scene in a Brothel

The Dresden painting *The Procuress* (ill. p. 23), on the other hand, is free of any
such inadequacies. Vermeer changed genres in this painting, dated 1656. Arthur
Wheelock has assumed that the artist was inspired to use this subject matter by
the painting of the same name by the Utrecht Caravaggist Dirck van Baburen
(1590–1624); it was owned by his mother-in-law, Maria Thins, and appears as a
reference on the walls of several of his interiors (ill. p. 22 bottom).

Vermeer's picture belongs in the category of "Bordeeltje," brothel pictures,
which was greatly valued as a sub-category in Dutch genre painting. The great
interest that was shown in such themes indicates that the public was finding a
way of compensating for an increasingly prudish moral code. These Bordeeltjes
derive to a large extent from paintings of the Prodigal Son (*filius prodigus*), who
is in the inn, frittering his money away on whores (Luke 15, 11 ff.) This scene
very frequently appeared in prints in the sixteenth century, in versions such as
those by Lucas van Leyden (1494–1533) and the *Sorgheloos* series by an anonymous artist (Amsterdam, 1541). Originally, Christ's parable of the Prodigal Son
was used to demonstrate the contrast between Catholic principles and the
Reformers' view of the principle of divine mercy, shown when the lost son is
received with loving forgiveness by his father.

The motif of the brothel proved fascinating; it is not surprising, therefore,
that it quickly developed into an independent genre. From a humanist point of
view, it was possible to combine it with the didactic warning that one should
learn from such paintings, how easily one could be fleeced in public houses.
Warnings against fraud, cheating, and theft also occur frequently in stories
about fools; an example is Sebastian Brant's *Narrenschiff* (*Ship of Fools*), which
appeared in 1494. These writings also warned of the consequences of alcoholism, because it reduced one's vigilance, and would ultimately lead the drinker
to poverty.

The majority of genre paintings were not simply naive depictions of reality,
but always conveyed norms and values in a way that altered what was happening. This painting is no exception, and the subject here is the problem of con-
trolling sensuousness, that one should always be vigilant and sober. The motif of
alcohol – or, to be precise, of drinking wine – is a central element of Vermeer's
painting. The table in the picture is parallel to the frame, and acts as a barrier
between the observer and the participants in the scene. It is covered by a carpet,
and a carafe is placed to the right. The young woman wearing the yellow jerkin
is holding a wine glass in her left hand, as is the reveller on the left side of the
picture; he is clothed in dark burgundy.

The actual theme here is that everything can be bought, including love. The
wine has brought colour to the young woman's cheeks, and she has opened her
hand to receive a coin in payment for her services from a cavalier, who is wearing a hat decorated with feathers and a vermilion jerkin. It has yet to be shown
to what extent this is a brothel scene in the narrower sense. A piece of lace work

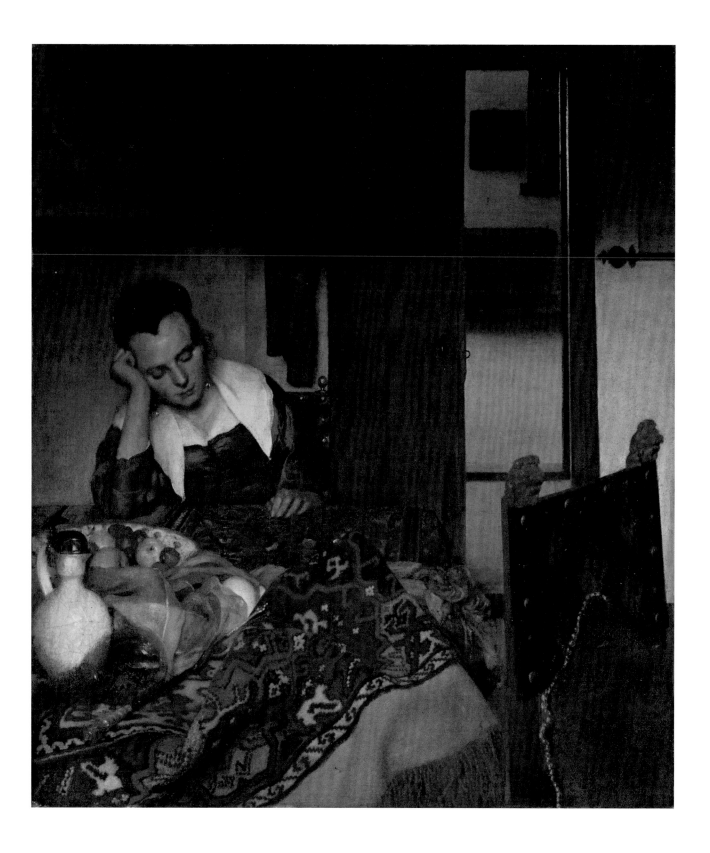

can just be recognised where it has been put down on the right on the table carpet, and this is a striking feature. It makes it possible to infer that this is most likely a domestic scene. In that case, what is happening here is that an extramarital love affair is being initiated with the help of the procuress, who is dressed in black; she is probably an old woman living in the vicinity, who has come to witness the successful conclusion to her efforts. Vermeer's picture, which gives us a close-up view of the scene, is restrained and semantically rather more open in structure when compared to other paintings on a similar theme, such as Frans van Mieris the Elder's *The Soldier and the Prostitute* (1658; ill. p. 22 top). They tend to fill out the plot with more detail, and occasionally include some quite graphic allusions; dogs are copulating in Mieris's painting.

A Drunken Girl Asleep at a Table

As can be seen from the carafe on the left of the picture, the theme of drinking wine is taken up again in this painting of a young woman, which is now in New York (ill. p. 24). A young woman, leaning her head against her right hand, is sitting opposite us at a table. The table is covered with a heavy oriental carpet, the foremost part of which is arranged in a disorderly fashion to form a pyramid. The girl is obviously asleep. Indeed, when the painting was sold in Amsterdam on 16 May 1696, it was given the title *Een dronke slafende Meyd aen een Tafel* (*A drunken girl asleep at a table*); when sold again in 1737 it was described as *Een slapent vrouwtje, van de Delfse van der Meer* (*A sleeping young woman, by Van der Meer of Delft*). If the elegant clothes are anything to go by, she is not a maid, but a *huisvrouw*, or in other words a wife who is in charge of the household.

Vermeer uses very few elements in his pictures, in contrast to Jan Steen, for example, who fills his pictures with a profusion of objects and (usually noisy) participants (ill. p. 9). The woman is isolated from anything that might be happening elsewhere. X-ray examination has shown that there were originally other elements in this painting which Vermeer later painted out: initially, there was a dog in the doorway, and a man in the room beyond. By painting out these narrative additions, he made his composition easier to interpret. The woman's gestures are not so clear, however. They could be considered signs of melancholy, like those of Mary in the earlier history painting. It is more likely, however, that this is a reference to the traditional motif of acedia, or sloth, which was frequently represented in this way.

In mediaeval theology, acedia was considered a vice, even a mortal sin. This was an age in which the authorities were constructing a rigid, ascetic work ethos, complete with norms which extended right into the home; for a wife to violate these norms must have seemed to be a direct violation of God's law. In the literature of seventeenth-century housefathers, it was expected that the "housemother," as the commander of the household, would be god-fearing and virtuous, a shining example of Christian virtues and a model for the riff-raff.

Acedia was frequently explained to be a consequence of alcoholism. In his painting *The Consequences of Immoderation* (c. 1663–65, London, National Gallery), Jan Steen depicted a woman who had drunk herself to sleep on wine. Sleeping means that she is neglecting her duties: the household is all topsy-turvy, the children are letting the cat nibble a pie, the maid is giving the parrot a drink of wine, and a couple of lovers are amusing themselves in the garden. So the sacred household order has been annulled. The acedia motif appears at a lower social level in Nicolaes Maes's painting *The Lazy Maid* (ill. p. 26). Here it is the maid who has made free with her master's wine and has therefore not been able

Samuel van Hoogstraten (attrib.)
The Slippers, 1660–65
Oil on canvas, 103 x 70 cm (40½ x 27½ in.)
Paris, Musée du Louvre

Situations where the observer is offered a view from one room, through an open door, into a neighbouring room were frequently found in paintings of Dutch interiors in the third quarter of the seventeenth century. Vermeer himself, in his early painting *A Maid Asleep* made use of such a view into a second room.

PAGE 24
A Maid Asleep, c. 1656/57
Oil on canvas, 87.6 x 76.5 cm (34½ x 30 in.)
New York, The Metropolitan Museum of Art, Bequest of Benjamin Altman, 1913

If the quality of the clothing is anything to go by, this is the lady of the house. The way she is supporting her head on her hand was a traditional motif which signified acedia, or sloth; here this is due to drunkenness, as the carafe of wine in the foreground tells us. This woman has been neglecting the household duties entrusted to her.

Nicolaes Maes
The Lazy Maid, 1655
Oil on wood, 70 x 53.3 cm (27½ x 21 in.)
London, The National Gallery

In this painting, it is the maid who has drunk
too much wine and is neglecting her duties.

to carry out her tasks. That this is the case is made clear by the untidy pile of crockery on the floor, and the cat, who is snatching away a plucked hen.

The intake of wine on the part of Vermeer's sleeping young woman evidently has something to do with an extramarital love affair. The man in the neighbouring room, who was later painted out, is not the only indication of this. The picture that is hanging on the wall over the woman is not a coincidence: it is a *clavis interpretandi*, giving us a clue as to the erotic context of the scene. It is difficult to make out, as it is in strong shadow. It has been possible to ascertain that Vermeer is making a reference here to one of Caesar van Everdingen's (c. 1616–1678) paintings, which depicts a putto, or small Eros, wearing a mask, which was a sign of pretence. Everdingen's picture goes back to an emblem of Otto van Veen's (*Amorum Emblemata*, Antwerp 1608), whose motto was "Love demands honesty."

Other items which indicate the erotic content of Vermeer's picture include the almost still-life bowl of fruit – the "fruits of evil" – and the egg, wrapped up in a cloth, which is a sign of something that should be avoided: unbridled libido. Vermeer must have known parts of classical literature which were frequently quoted by seventeenth-century authors, such as Jacob Cats, who were keen to educate the people. According to them, women were forbidden to drink wine, as drunkenness led to whoring. One classical saying was repeatedly cited: "Mulier si temetum biberit domi ut adulteram puniunta" ("If a woman drinks wine at home, she should be punished as an adulteress").

Vermeer was starting to place great emphasis on geometric compositions when he painted this picture. Something appears here which was to become typical of most of his interiors: rooms which are arranged parallel to the picture, something which can be seen by the back walls, and also by the tables placed, like barriers, horizontally to the frame. This enabled him to avoid the strong distortions of perspective caused by using a camera obscura (cf. ill. p. 16). The effect which this in turn caused was a strong tendency to align the surfaces in the room so that doorframes, mirrors and pictures, tables and other furnishings take on an almost abstract tectonic and geometric structure.

PAGE 27
Detail of *A Maid Asleep* (ill. p. 24)

The Temptations of Love

Seduction and Wine

The theme of the girl asleep was taken up again by Vermeer in his painting *Cavalier and Young Woman* (ill. p. 32). In the (probably) earlier painting (ill. p. 24), the situation appears to have been freed from the narrative context; in the latter, the process of seducing someone with the help of wine is depicted quite bluntly. We see the partial profile of a cavalier who is wearing a wide-brimmed hat, and is sitting, in deep shadow, in the foreground on the left, with his hand on his hip and his back partly turned to us. He is talking to a young woman who is smiling back at him; she is wearing a white headscarf and is lit up by the light streaming in through the open window. The rhetorical gesture of her open left hand underlines the nature of the conversation here. Nowhere else in Vermeer's pictures is there such a great difference between the sizes of the man and the woman; it is caused by the sharply shortened perspective of the room. The man dominates the scene; it is he who is trying to use wine to make the young woman submissive. The contrast between light and shadow could even contain unconscious (or perhaps intentional?) psychological symbolism. It is likely that the woman, who is lit up by the sun, embodies the principle of purity, and that she is, so to speak, the victim of the man's dark and sinister machinations.

Vermeer's love of maps (cf. ills. p. 33) is expressed in his reproduction of one on the back wall of the room; maps, like the pictures he included, were of particular significance in his paintings. This map was designed in 1620 by Balthasar Florisz. van Berckenrode (1591–1645) and published by Willem Jansz. Blaeu (1571–1638) shortly afterwards. The Latin inscription reads, "NOVA ET ACCVRATA TOTIVS HOLLANDIAE WESTFRISIAEQ(VE) TOPOGRAPHIA," and shows that the map covers Holland and the West Frisian Islands; in contrast to modern cartographic practice, the map is on an east-west, not a north-south, axis. Maps were still an expensive luxury in the middle of the seventeenth century, but they were also considered a sign of humanistic knowledge. To refer to such maps was frequently a device on the part of Vermeer by which to allude to contemporary political situations. Thus this picture, with the soldier, could be an allusion to the Anglo-Dutch War of 1652–54, during which Admiral Michiel Adriaens-zoon de Ruyter won many great victories for the Republic of the United Netherlands.

Gerard ter Borch
A Cavalier Offering a Lady a Glass of Wine,
c. 1660
Oil on board, 41.3 x 32.1 cm (16¼ x 12¾ in.)
London, The Royal Collection,
Her Majesty Queen Elizabeth II

PAGE 28
Detail of *The Girl with the Wineglass*
(ill. p. 31)

Frans Hals
Tieleman Roosterman, 1634
Oil on canvas, 117 x 87 cm (46 x 34¼ in.)
The Cleveland Museum of Art

The husband's portrait on the wall in *The Girl with the Wineglass* reminiscent of Frans Hals's portraits.

PAGE 31
The Girl with the Wineglass, c. 1659/60
Oil on canvas, 78 x 67.5 cm (30¾ x 26½ in.)
Brunswick, Herzog Anton Ulrich-Museum

The woman is looking towards us questioningly; the man in the centre, who is trying to get her to drink, seems to be acting as a matchmaker between her and the gentleman seated sideways in the background. The portrait on the wall is probably of her husband. It is no accident that, though he is not actually present, he should be there in this picture, looking at the young woman.

The Glass of Wine (ill. pp. 34/35) has a similar theme to the *Cavalier and Young Woman* (ill. p. 32); it differs, however, in that it portrays its characters at a greater distance from our own point of view. They are not cut off by the lower frame of the picture, a device which would make them seem extremely close; instead, they can be seen in the centre of the room. The layout of the room in particular the chequered pattern of the tiled floor, was evidently inspired by Pieter de Hooch.

The man is offering wine to the woman – as an aphrodisiac, to lower her resistance. His hand is clutching the handle of a white carafe that appears as a significant leitmotif on several of Vermeer's paintings (cf. ill. pp. 31, 34/35, 38/39, 47). Here it is placed squarely in the middle of the picture, and cannot be overlooked. The man is appraising the young woman with his gaze, and she has already raised the shimmering glass to her mouth; it half covers her face, almost like a mask. The scene has evidently been preceded by a musical divertimento to get them into the right mood. This is suggested by the lute which has been placed on the chair, and the sheet music lying on the Persian carpet on the table.

This room makes a gloomier impression, in contrast to the one the *Cavalier and Young Woman* are in. The reason for this is that the lower part of the window in the background is shuttered, and a curtain is drawn across the upper part. As in the case of the *Woman with a Balance* (ill. p. 61), this is not without its deeper significance. It is probably a reference to a Biblical passage, Proverbs 4,19: "The way of the wicked is as dark as night." So something is occurring here that has good cause to shun the light. A German encyclopaedia, Zedler's *Universal-Lexikon* (Halle/Leipzig, 1734, vol. 8, col. 339), associates dark rooms with adultery, and quotes Job 24, 15: "Others of them hate the light", "The eye of the adulterer watches for twilight, 'No-one will see me,' he mutters."

The partly opened window has a particular moral meaning which acts as a commentary on the scene, as it were. On it there can be seen – next to the arms of Jannetje Vogel, who died in 1621 and whose first marriage was to Vermeer's neighbour Moses J. Nederveen – a symbolic motif which has its origins in an illustration in Gabriel Rollenhagen's 1611 *Book of Emblems* (ill. p. 34). It concerns the personification of *Temperantia*, or Temperance, one of the cardinal virtues, together with its attributes, the Level (symbolising good deeds) and the Bridle (symbolising emotional control). The window is directly in the woman's line of vision, and is her opposite, its purpose being to serve as a warning.

The theme of Temperance crops up again in Vermeer's Brunswick painting *The Girl with the Wineglass* (ill. p. 31), and the purpose of this picture is clearly similar. The scene does differ from the Berlin picture *The Glass of Wine* (ill. pp. 34/35), however, in that not one but two men are present. The seduction seems to be even more intensive, and the man in the centre is bending down and talking to the young woman; she is wearing an elegant, full satin dress and looks rather embarrassed and unsure of herself. While the young woman in the Berlin painting has already raised her glass to her mouth, her counterpart in the Brunswick painting still seems somewhat reticent and uncertain.

The drink need not necessarily have been wine. It could also be a love potion (Lat. *poculum amatorium*, Fr. *philtre d'amour*), such as is frequently mentioned in seventeenth-century medical writings; Jan Baptista van Helmont said that it caused "the natural essences of life to surge."[4]

The effect could be one of two things: either excessive, foolish love, or a paralysing melancholy. The man seated at the table, leaning his head on his hand, has evidently also drunk some, because his attitude is one of melancholy. It is likely

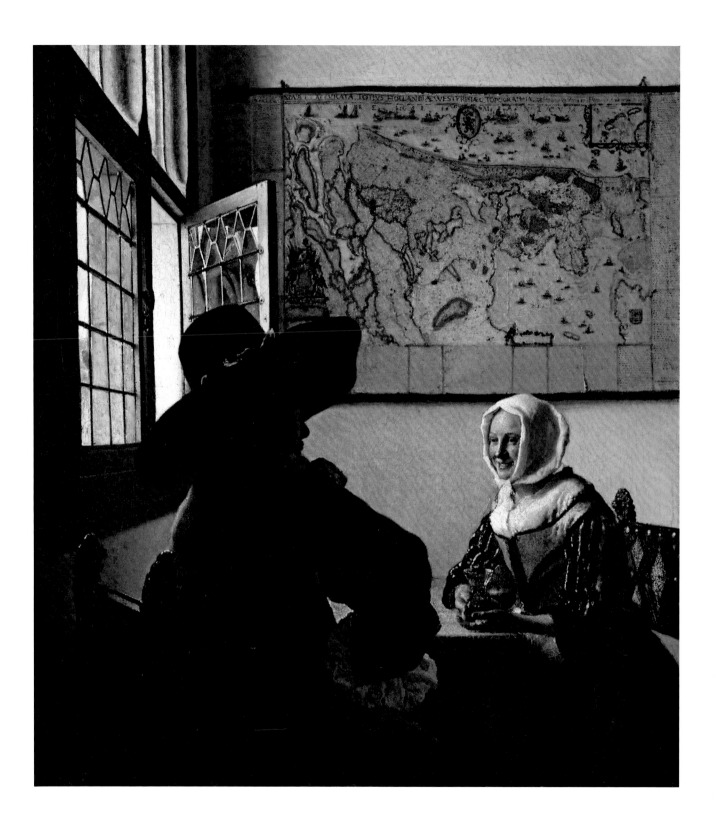

PAGE 32
Cavalier and Young Woman, c. 1657–59
Oil on canvas, 50.5 x 46 cm (20 x 18 in.)
New York, The Frick Collection

FROM TOP LEFT TO BOTTOM RIGHT
Details of *The Art of Painting* (ill. p. 85),
Woman in Blue Reading a Letter (ill. p. 52),
Woman with a Lute (ill. p. 45) and
Young Woman with a Water Pitcher (ill. p. 69)

Vermeer's love of maps becomes apparent in the way he decorates his interiors. The role of maps was twofold: on the one hand, they indicated wealth (in the seventeenth century, maps were an expensive luxury); on the other hand, they refer to a good level of education. Cartography was still a new science, but was beginning to be held in high regard.

Gabriel Rollenhagen
Serva modum, 1611
Illustration of *Temperance in Nucleus
Emblematum*, Cologne, 1611

The inscription on the emblem is "serva
modum" (Be moderate). The Level (symbolising
good deeds) and the Bridle (symbolising emotional control) are attributes that often accompanied personifications of Temperance.

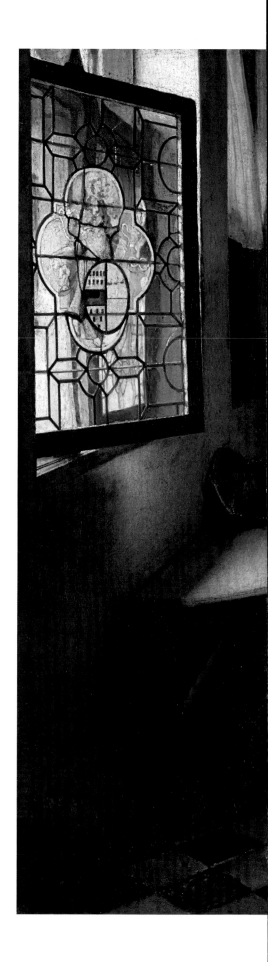

The Glass of Wine, c. 1658–66
Oil on canvas, 65 x 77 cm (25½ x 30¼ in.)
Berlin, Staatliche Museen zu Berlin,
Gemäldegalerie

Like *The Girl with the Wine Glass* (ill. p. 31),
this seduction scene contains an open window
which features the warning figure of Temperance.

Otto van Veen
Perfectus Amor Est Nisi ad Unum, 1608
Copper engraving, illustration of Cupid
in *Amorum Emblemata*, Antwerp, 1608

The motto on the emblem is: "There can only
be perfect love for one person."

that the man in the centre is acting as a matchmaker, and that in the absence of the husband (because on the wall is the portrait of a man, and it is no coincidence that he is looking down at the woman). What is taking place here is the initiation of a secret love affair, "clam et absente marito," or secretly and in the absence of the husband, as it was phrased in legal texts of the time that dealt with adultery.

A peeled orange in *The Girl with the Wineglass* (ill. p. 31) lies on a silver dish next to a jug which has been placed on a white cloth in an arrangement which is almost like a still life; the purpose of the lemon was to reduce the effect of love potions.

The Power of Music

The Berlin painting *The Glass of Wine* (ill. pp. 34/35) has already tied in the motif of love potions with that of music; this combination appears even more forcefully in *Young Woman Interrupted at Music* (ill. pp. 38/39). A young woman wearing a red jacket and white headcloth has just laid her lute and sheet music down on the table, in order to start reading a letter which a man has just given to her. She gazes towards us questioningly, uncertain whether she should read this secret message – it is probably a love letter. Once again the theme of the painting is erotic, as is suggested by the barely recognisable scene in the faded picture on the back wall, which is based on a painting by Caesar van Everdingen. It features Cupid, who is holding up a love letter.

This picture within a picture also appears in another of Vermeer's paintings, *Lady Standing at a Virginal* (detail p. 37 and ill. p. 42). Everdingen's painting derives from an emblem by Otto van Veen (ill. p. 36), which bore the motto "Perfectus Amor Est Nisi ad Unum" (There can only be perfect love for one person). So the young woman shown here is in the process, against the expectations of society, of being unfaithful to her husband. The birdcage on the wall is a sign of how she should be behaving; in books of emblems, such as that of Daniel Heinsius (*Emblemata amatoria*, Leiden 1615), a birdcage symbolised the willing captivity of love. Heinsius's motto ran: "For I have bound myself" (Perch' io stesso mi strinsi).[5]

The connection of love and music was also a central theme in the London painting *The Music Lesson* (ill. p. 47). The overall impression here, however, is much more restrained and refined. The scene is set inside an upper middle class home. It is not seen close by, but is taking place further away from the observer, in the background by the rear wall of the room. A young woman wearing a vermilion skirt with a white blouse and black outer garment is standing there, playing on the narrow keyboard of a virginal. She is seen from behind, and is therefore anonymous, but her face can be seen in the mirror hanging over the virginal. Though the view from behind might lead one to expect otherwise, she is looking to one side, towards a young man. He is wearing an elegant black robe with a white lace collar and white cuffs, and a rapier is fastened to his sash, a sure sign of social importance.

X-ray examinations have shown that Vermeer originally painted the woman's head turned further towards the man. This shows that Vermeer was attempting to create a more balanced picture by removing the more obvious references to the theme, and that he carried out further corrections in order to broaden the significance of the scene. In this way the visual attraction of the painting becomes all the more intense. This is true not only of the muted colour harmonies, but also – indeed, all the more so – of the geometrical structures, which are of crucial importance for the composition. As in so many of his works, Vermeer heavily accentuates horizontals parallel to the picture frame – such as the beams of the ceiling, the oblongs of the virginal, the mirror, the picture on the right, and the table which, interposed like a barrier between ourselves and the subject on the right, has a heavy Persian carpet draped across it and reaching to the floor, on top of which is the familiar white carafe standing on the equally familiar silver plate. The diamond-shaped pattern of the floor tiles, which comprises white tiles set in a lattice of black ones, also pays homage to geometry.

To just what extent Vermeer was intentionally using geometric shapes in his compositions – and some scholars see pre-Mondrianesque trends in pictures such as this – will remain open to debate. It is striking, though, that after the middle of the seventeenth century geometry gained importance in philosophical and scientific circles. One need only think of the subtitle of Spinoza's *Ethics*: "ordine geometrico demonstrata" (arrange according to geometric principles). At that time, which witnessed the growth of the exact sciences, the ideal of geometry stood for clarity and demonstrability, and for methodical stringency in proof. Its history stretched back to antiquity, to such early masters as Pythagoras, when geometry and music were seen as close kin, both touching upon cosmic laws.

Vermeer's virginal, and the viola da gamba laid at an angle on the floor, may therefore embody an allusion to the harmony or music of the spheres. But music was also thought to possess therapeutic value, as the inscription on the virginal makes plain: MVSICA LETITIAE CO[ME?]S / MEDICINA DOLOR[VM?] ("Music is the accompanist of joy, a remedy for sorrow"). This statement could be traced back to Pythagoras, who reputedly said that the harmonies of music could moderate and pacify agitations of spirit, and influence the emotions.

The Concert (ill. p. 40) distances what is taking place from us by moving the action to the rear wall of the room. Two pictures are hanging on it; one is a pastoral landscape, the other is the painting of *The Procuress*, by the Utrecht Caravaggist Dirck van Baburen (ill. p. 22 bottom), which Vermeer often includes in his own paintings. A harpsichord is positioned close to the wall, and we see a young woman in profile playing it. She is accompanied by a man playing a lute (only the end of the fingerboard with the tuning keys is visible); his back is turned towards us, and he is sitting beside the harpsichord facing the Arcadian landscape on the lid of the instrument, on a chair which is placed at an angle to the room. A somewhat older woman, who is singing the vocal accompaniment, is standing next to them. Further musical instruments, grouped like a still life, are on the floor and the sturdy oak table on the left. Vermeer particularly liked stringed instruments (the harpsichord may be included in the family), and they belonged to a long tradition of musical symbols of proportion and harmony.

In classical times, the cithara was a stringed instrument that was held in high regard. It was considered noble enough to be dedicated to Apollo, and this is in sharp contrast to the flute (*aulos*), which was dedicated to Dionysus and, due to its association with orgies, was considered to be a most primitive instrument. Such musical concepts, which had been passed on by humanistic traditions, were still current in the seventeenth century. Nor should we forget the theory of emotions prompted by music; this had a long tradition and was summarised by Johannes Tinctoris (1435–1511). This theory held that the task of music was not only to praise God, but also to dispel melancholy, to exalt the spirits on this earth, to heal the sick, to entice love, and to make life together more pleasant. These last

Detail of *Lady Standing at a Virginal*
(ill. p. 42)

Vermeer repeatedly gives us hints as to how we should interpret his paintings. For instance, the cupid holding the playing card in this painting within a painting raises doubts as to the virginity of the woman at the virginal.

Young Woman Interrupted at Music,
c. 1659–61
Oil on canvas, 39.3 x 44.4 cm (15½ x 17½ in.)
New York, The Frick Collection

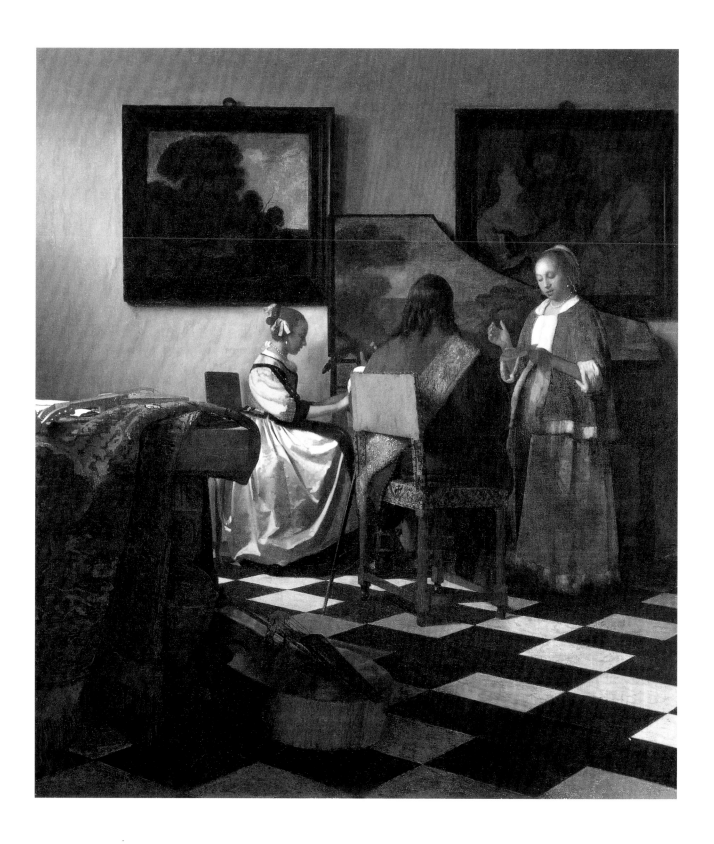

two aspects, in particular, were those that Vermeer and other Dutch genre painters (such as Gerard ter Borch) were alluding to in their house-music scenes.

As well as duets and trios, Vermeer frequently painted solo performers, without exception women. *Lady Standing at a Virginal* (ill. p. 42), which Thoré-Bürger bought, can be dated to his late phase (approximately 1670–72). We see a relatively small spatial area. Once again, there are two paintings hanging on the wall, one a small gold-framed landscape (perhaps by Allaert van Everdingen or Jan Wijnants), the other Caesar van Everdingen's *Cupid*, which we have already seen as a clavis interpretandi in *Young Woman Interrupted at Music* (ill. pp. 38/39).

Cupid is holding up a card, a gesture which plainly relates to the young, seemingly naive woman. Structurally, this feature recalls the smirking figures in Dutch genre paintings, whose victims do not notice what is going on since the gestures are made purely to assist our understanding. These gestures derived from performances of comedies and farces, where pointed remarks and innuendoes addressed to the audience, outside the frame of the action, were the order of the day. We have already seen that Vermeer is using Everdingen's picture as a means of referring to Otto van Veen's emblem (ill. p. 36) granting perfect love for one person only – the husband, of course. The instrument the woman is playing, a virginal, suggests through its name her virgin status – though Cupid may be ironically questioning it.

The subject of virginity preoccupied the authors of didactic and legal tracts at that period. In a society whose patriarchal structures were being consolidated, there was much eager debate of whether women should enter marriage intact. Alongside this debate on social norms, however, there was always the realisation that unbending moral precepts had but little connection with the real world. Dutch genre painters, who took the authority of Cicero in conceiving of their pictures as visual comedies, were notably sceptical, portraying the prevailing morality in their paintings while simultaneously subverting it with irony.

Vermeer's second picture of a woman at a virginal (ill. p. 43), which critics assign to his final period, is similar in its deployment of motifs to the *Lady Standing at a Virginal* (ill. p. 42). The girl is seated at the virginal, gazing sideways at us. Her head and arms have not been painted with great attention to individuality, and even the folds of her clothing are only slightly nuanced areas of colour with a few unsubtle highlights. The viola da gamba in the foreground, leant against the marble-patterned virginal, suggests that a second person has just been present, that their duet may, in other words, have included a little flirtation. Dirck van Baburen's *Procuress*, the painting on the wall, underlines this innuendo. Blue curtains have been drawn across the window, darkening the room and implying that this secret rendezvous does not welcome the light of day.

The window in *Woman with a Lute* (ill. p. 45) has also been shaded. Light enters only at the bottom, below the curtain, brightening the yellow of the young woman's right sleeve and part of her collar. Her forehead, too, is lit by this indirect light. Her pearl earring (revealed in 1944, when the painting was cleaned) and her pearl necklace are gleaming.

The girl is sitting behind a table, in front of which stands a chair in dark silhouette. She seems to be tuning her instrument, and is leaning forward a little, her head inclined to listen. Since the Renaissance, the lute had been the attribute or sign of music par excellence in symbolic works; at times it also represented

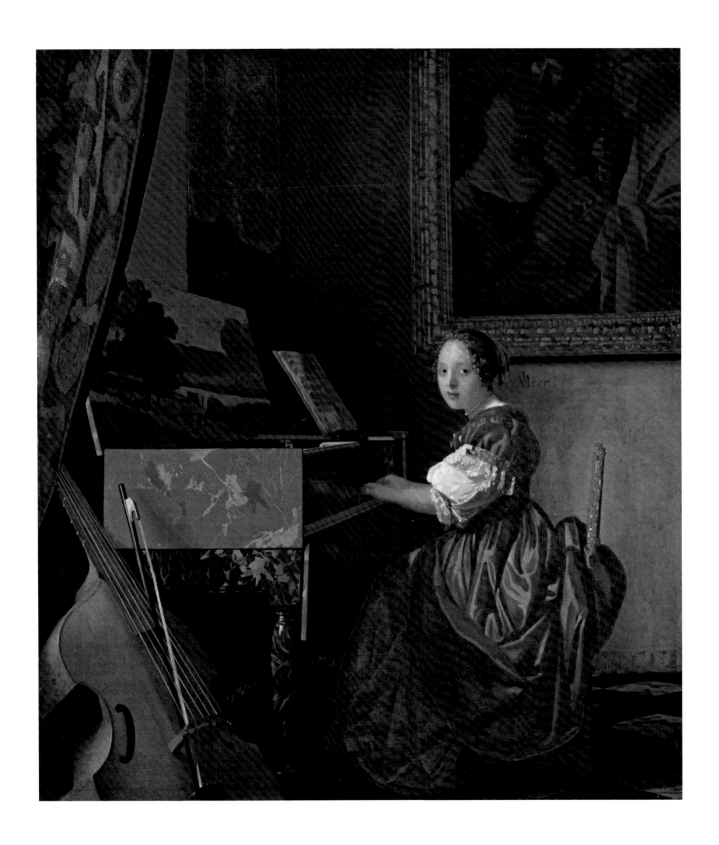

PAGE 45
Woman with a Lute, c. 1662–64
Oil on canvas, 51.4 x 45.7 cm (20¼ x 18 in.)
New York, The Metropolitan Museum of Art,
Bequest of Collis P. Huntington, 1900

The pearl earring and necklace came to light
when the painting was cleaned in 1944. They
gleam prettily in the light.

one of the five senses, hearing. A quiet instrument, it was most suitable for indoor playing, and hardly at all for concerts in the open. It was primarily an instrument for private solo performance, and thus had a certain intimacy.

The same was true of the guitar, the main subject in a late Vermeer, *The Guitar Player* (ill. p. 46). Again, the room has been somewhat darkened. In the corner, books are piled on a table, while in the foreground a young woman is playing the guitar. This divertimento is doubtless being played to encourage thoughts and feelings of love. These feelings are at odds with the reading of books, which lie neglected; it is impossible to be certain what books they are, but it is a fair guess that the Bible and Catechism are among them, since these were recommended to young ladies for moral guidance.

Vermeer painted one more picture of a girl alone with her instrument, *Girl with a Flute* (ill. p. 73). In her left hand she is holding a flute, an instrument traditionally with erotic associations. In the story of Hercules at the parting of the ways (Xenophon: *Memorabilia* 2, 1–22) – which was repeatedly painted by Renaissance artists, since it dealt with the polarity of virtue and vice – the flute was a symbol of sensuality. As we have already seen, it was used in the cult of Dionysus or Bacchus, the God of Wine and of unrestrained libido.

Crispin de Passe
Amor Docet Musicam
Etching for Gabriel Rollenhagen's *Nucleus Emblematum*, Cologne, 1611

Amor was traditionally depicted holding a lute.

PAGE 46
The Guitar Player, c. 1669–72
Oil on canvas, 51.4 x 45 cm (20¼ x 17¾ in.)
London, Kenwood House,
The Iveagh Bequest

PAGE 47
The Music Lesson (A Woman at a Virginal with a Gentleman), c. 1662–64
Oil on canvas, 74 x 64.5 cm (29¼ x 25½ in.)
London, Royal Collection,
Her Majesty Queen Elizabeth II

Secret Yearnings

Love Letters

Vermeer's *Young Woman Reading a Letter* (detail p. 48 and ill. p. 51), now in Dresden, is usually considered to be an early work. It shows a young woman at an open window, reading with great inner tension and attentiveness a love letter that has been addressed to her. We see her in profile, but her face is reflected at a slight angle in the lightly coloured, uneven glass panes of the leaded window (the same feature occurs in the picture *Cavalier and Young Woman*, ill. p. 32). The fact that it is open does of course superficially serve to increase the amount of light falling into the rather dark room, but in another sense it represents the woman's longing to extend her domestic sphere, and her desire for contact with the outside world, from which she, as a housewife forced to keep to her society's norms, is largely isolated. This longing to break free from isolation is occasionally also a feature of Pieter de Hooch's paintings, such as the one which features a woman standing in an entryway and looking out onto the street (ill. p. 13).

The bowl of fruit in Vermeer's *A Young Woman Reading a Letter*, which is lying on the folds of the table rug, is a symbol of extramarital relations, which broke the vow of chastity. Such a relationship is being planned or continued by means of this letter, and the apples and peaches (malum persicum) are intended to remind us of Eve's transgression. The yellowish-green silk curtain and rail is an artistic piece of bravura on the part of Vermeer. It is difficult to decide whether it is to be seen as part of the picture, a curtain in the room, like others that Vermeer uses, pushed to one side to reveal what is going oh, or whether – as in Rembrandt's 1646 picture of the *Holy Family* (Kassel, Gemäldegalerie Alte Meister) – it is meant to create the illusion of a protective curtain hung in front of the painting.

Another woman who is lost in thought, completely engrossed in reading the letter she has just received, is the *Woman in Blue Reading a Letter* (ill. p. 52). Like the girl in the Dresden painting, she is facing the window, which is not visible, though the brightness of the wall on the left would suggest the presence of such a source of light. The woman may well be pregnant.[6] If that is indeed the case, her reading of this letter would be a moral contradiction of the respectability of marriage, which, according to contemporary writings on marriage, was an institution that was designed to ensure the reproduction of the species and did not allow for "unchaste, lascivious thoughts."

Gerard ter Borch
The Letter Writer, c. 1655
Oil on board, 39 x 29.5 cm (15¼ x 11½ in.)
The Hague, Koninklijk Kabinet
van Schilderijen Mauritshuis

PAGE 48
Detail of *A Young Woman Reading a Letter*
(ill. p. 51)

Open windows frequently have a figurative meaning in Vermeer's paintings. Taken together with the letter, which the girl is holding, this motif represents the desire to break free from the restrictions of the home and make contact with the outside world.

Gerard Houckgeest
The Interior of the Oude Kerk in Delft,
c. 1654 (?)
Oil on board, 49 x 41 cm (19¼ x 16¼ in.)
Amsterdam, Rijksmuseum

The use of drapery is frequently found in the
work of Delft painters in the mid-seventeenth
century, and it was especially favoured by archi-
tectural painters such as Gerard Houckgeest.
However, whereas in his work a curtain in the
foreground and a view beyond of the church interior would effectively represent two distinct
levels of reality, in Vermeer's picture *A Young
Woman Reading a Letter* the curtain and the
figure beyond are rendered on the same scale.

PAGE 51
*A Young Woman Reading a Letter
(The Letter Reader)*, c. 1657
Oil on canvas, 83 x 64.5 cm (32¾ x 25½ in.)
Dresden, Staatliche Kunstsammlungen,
Gemäldegalerie Alte Meister

Speculation in earlier works on Vermeer that the woman depicted here could
well be his wife, who went through a large number of pregnancies, is immaterial
when we interpret this painting. Even if Catharina Bolnes was the artist's model,
the painting should not be viewed as a biographical document; what is being
portrayed and discussed here is a more general social problem. As in the painting of the *Woman with a Balance* (ill. p. 61), or the *Woman with a Pearl Necklace*
(ill. p. 59), the box of pearls is a symbol of Superbia, or vanity, because this
woman is dressing up for her lover.

The woman wearing the yellow, ermine-trimmed jacket (ill. p. 54), who is
herself writing a love letter with a goose quill as she smiles at the observer, is also
smartly dressed up. A pearl necklace with a yellow ribbon is lying right next to
the letter paper, and it is also possible to make out a jewellery box and an ink set.
In contrast to the picture *Woman in Blue Reading a Letter*, which presents the
theme of vanity rather discreetly, the theme is quite unmistakable here. The inclusion of the decorative ribbons and pearl earrings is intended to show the
woman's craving to be smart and be admired (cf. ill. pp. 56/57) – though pearls
can also have a more positive meaning in Vermeer's art (cf. ill. p. 61). For the artist, they were a welcome opportunity to show off his talents in creating the gra-
dations of yellow, which are continued in darker tones in the jacket. According
to Andrea Alciatis's *Emblemata* (Lyons, 1550, ill. p. 128), yellow is a colour which
is "amantibus et scortis aptus," or "appropriate for lovers and whores."[7]

The woman's fashionable appearance and the objects on the table are repeated in Vermeer's *Mistress and Maid* (ill. p. 55). A new feature in this scene is the
maid, who is stepping forward out of the dark background to give the woman a
letter; the latter, who has just written a few lines, is obviously hesitant to accept
it. It seems to throw her into confusion, and she is beginning to have scruples
about whether she should let herself in on this adventure or not. It may be that
what she is writing in her own letter, and the content of the message that she has
yet to read, are at odds. The maid's expression makes it obvious that she is in on
this secret affair. She is acting as a silent go-between, and enjoys the confidence
of her mistress.

The relationship between the mistress and maid in *A Lady Writing a Letter
with Her Maid* (ill. p. 58) is of a similar nature. The scene is different in that both
characters are turned fully towards the observer; the maid is standing with her
arms folded, waiting for the letter which the woman, dressed in a white blouse
and white cap decorated with pearls, is writing eagerly. A seal, which has fallen
off the table, is lying at the front on the floor. The maid is looking at the window,
which features the only just recognisable Allegory of Temperance familiar from
other paintings by Vermeer (ill. pp. 34/35). It serves as a warning to the woman
to act moderately and keep her emotions under control.

The picture on the wall shows the finding of the infant Moses, who had been
set adrift on the Nile (Exodus 2, 1–10). This picture also appears, smaller, in *The
Astronomer* (ill. p. 78), now in Paris. It is a reference to secret love affairs. In the
seventeenth century, the story of Moses probably reminded people of child
abandonment. As Pierre Chaunu and Pierre Goubert have shown, this was a
common practice amongst women who, in the face of draconian punishments,
had to cover up the existence of illegitimate "children of sin."[8] This is confirmed,
for instance, by the "Recherches statistiques sur la ville de Paris," carried out
after 1680. It was a period that saw the norms of marriage becoming more rigid,
the demands of monogamy more imperative; and to suit the instincts and native
sensuality of the individual to the behaviour expected of him or her was a task

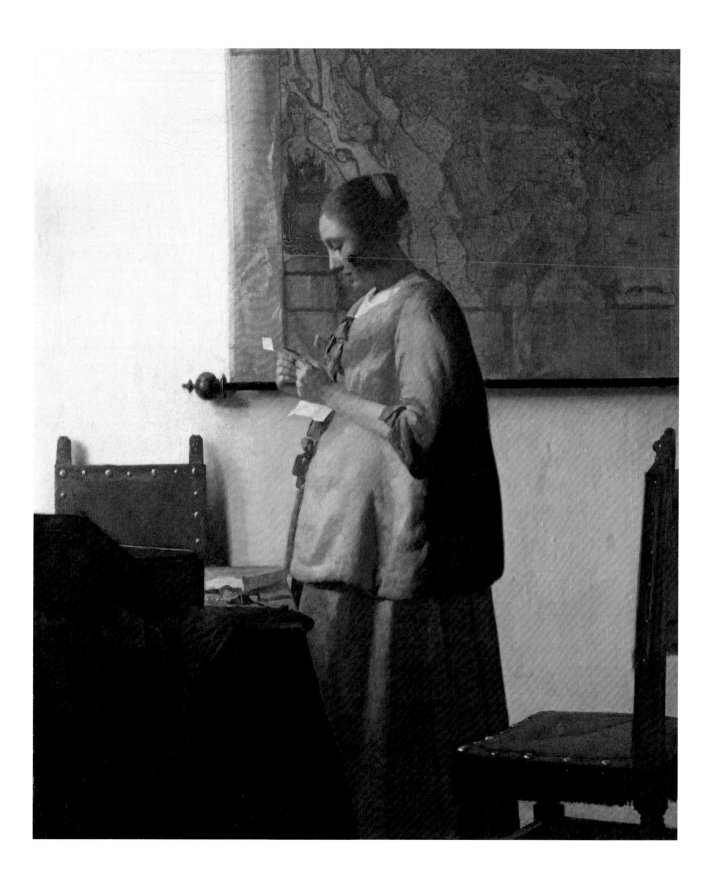

scarcely to be accomplished. The very high number of paintings that deal with extramarital relations show that it was difficult to impose proper monogamous behaviour from above.

Though the love-letter motif may at first glance appear an innocuous, anecdotal thing, then, it was in fact anything but. The contemporary literature of jurisprudence declared that *litterae amatoriae* (on which dissertations were written) were a proper subject of legal enquiry. The lawyers would aim to determine whether such letters implied a promise of marriage or (if one correspondent was already married) adultery. The level of educated literacy was rising among the prosperous bourgeoisie, and with it exchanges of letters; and many women were able to commit their feelings to paper. From a legal point of view, of course, this represented a serious risk, since written documents could be used as evidence.[9]

Vermeer returned again to the love-letter theme in the small-format Amsterdam painting *The Love Letter* (ill. p. 60). Again, the maid is the intimate confidante of the lady of the house. We see them from a dark hallway in which a map can dimly be made out on the wall, while on the right a musical score has been left on a chair beneath a curtain. The lady of the house is seated by a fireplace in a living room, gazing questioningly at her maid, who has just delivered a letter. The mandolin she is holding in her lap suggests that the lady has been tuning in musically to thoughts of love (cf. Crispin de Passe's emblem *Amor Docet Musicam*, ill. p. 44). In Dutch genre painting, fireplaces often stood metaphorically for the fiery passion of love. The marine painting on the wall behind her, showing a rough sea, suggests that the lady's passions have been agitated. The laundry basket, the embroidery cushion on the floor, and the broom by the door all betoken domestic duties neglected by the lady.

Pearl Jewellery

Woman with a Pearl Necklace (ill. p. 59) returns to the conflict of virtue and vice, but here the moral address is so discreet and muted that we scarcely feel it to be intended at all. A young (and perhaps pregnant) woman, wearing an ermine-trimmed yellow jacket, is seen in profile looking into a small mirror on the wall at left, which, with the yellow-curtained window, is rendered in sharp perspective. She has put on a pearl necklace, the tapes of which she is holding; and the subject of the painting is manifestly vanity, as the powder brush on the sturdy tabletop already suggests. The note lying beside the brush may well be meant to hint that she is putting on her finery for a lover.

Pearls, or pearl necklaces, carry a negative symbolic charge in the critique of vanitas, as we see, for example, in a thematically related illustration in Gérard de Lairesse's *Groot Schilderboek* (Amsterdam, 1707, vol I, pp. 188–93), where the personification of vanity is taking a pearl necklace from a jewellery box. The main argument in favour of the vanity interpretation is the mirror, an indispensable prop in toilette scenes, such as Frans van Mieris's *Young Lady before a Mirror* (ill. p. 62), in which the lady is admittedly far more magnificently dressed up than in Vermeer's work.

The motif on the leaded windows cannot be precisely made out. As in Vermeer's picture *The Girl with the Wineglass* (ill. p. 31), it may be another treatment of the subject of temperance. That is, it may represent an ethical contrast intended as a warning to a woman in danger of violating social norms: instead of leading a modest, contented and simple life, she seems to be falling prey to narcissism and the wish to be admired.

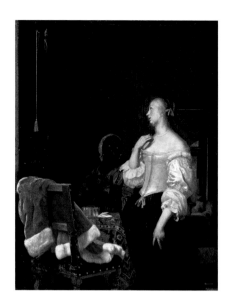

Frans van Mieris the Elder
Young Lady before a Mirror, c. 1662
Oil on board, 30 x 23 cm (11¾ x 9 in.)
Berlin, Staatliche Museen zu Berlin,
Gemäldegalerie

Pearls are again the subject in *Woman with a Balance* (ill. p. 61). The woman is carefully holding the scales in her right hand to balance them, and resting her left on the tabletop in order to concentrate. The room has been darkened by a curtain drawn across the window at the back left, where a strip of daylight can be seen. The pale light that enters the room is diffuse; but, since the source of light is at the top left, the visual space is divided diagonally into a brighter and a more shadowy area. The shadowy area becomes quite impenetrably dark in places, especially at the front left, where we can hardly make out what the objects in the painting are. Against this gloom, the pearls taken from the boxes are a sparkling highlight.

The picture on the wall behind the woman is a Last Judgement. The apocalyptic scene is an eschatological appeal to the conscience of the woman, plainly bearing a semantic relation to her thoughts and actions. On the Day of Judgement, as Christian teaching familiarly has it, good and evil will be sundered and the Blessed separated from the Damned. Christ, in his capacity as judge, will either grant the soul eternal peace, or damn it to the everlasting torments of hell.

Since the composition of this painting is closely related to that of the Berlin *Woman with a Pearl Necklace* (ill. p. 59) – both pictures featuring a mirror on the wall and the props of vanity on the table – it is tempting to interpret the action of this woman wary of the daylight in terms of vanitas. However, the action of weighing is ambivalent. Indeed, we may almost feel the woman's action echoes that of the weighing of the souls of the Resurrected (Job 31, 6). The balancing of the scales may therefore be intended in a psychological or ethical sense. Either way, there is an ambiguity of feeling in the motif. It has been pointed out that the scales are empty, and that therefore the woman's decision to forego all worldly finery has already been taken.

PAGE 60
The Love Letter, c. 1669/70
Oil on canvas, 44 x 38 cm (17¼ x 15 in.)
Amsterdam, Rijksmuseum

PAGE 61
Woman with a Balance, c. 1663/64
Oil on canvas, 40.3 x 35.6 cm (16 x 14 in.)
Washington, D.C., National Gallery of Art,
Widener Collection

The painting of the Day of Judgement on the wall takes on the role of a commentary on the woman weighing pearls. On the Day of Judgement, Christ will weigh the souls of the Blessed and the Damned; in the face of that, this fixation on earthly possessions appears empty and vain.

PAGE 63
Detail of ***Woman with a Pearl Necklace***,
(ill. p. 59)

Leading by Example

Women and Virtue

The overwhelming majority of Vermeer's paintings that depict women conform to the basic trend in Dutch genre painting, in that they criticise vice. It was their goal to educate people to behave "virtuously" – in other words to conform to norms of thought and behaviour – and to do this by depicting, in a comic manner, characters behaving wrongly.

The opposite of this is to educate by presenting the official code of behaviour by means of an *exemplum virtutis* (model of virtue); this method was seldom used. Only three of Vermeer's paintings have this purpose clearly in mind.

The most famous of these is probably *The Milkmaid* (ill. p. 67). It was valued highly right from the start, as is shown by the price (175 guilders) which this small picture fetched when the paintings in Vermeer's estate were sold in 1696. In 1719, the painting was even described with the words, "The famous milkmaid by Vermeer of Delft, artistic" (Het vermaerde Melkmeysje, door Vermeer van Delft, konstig).

Servants were normally portrayed in Dutch paintings as being lazy, as is shown by Nicolaes Maes's *The Lazy Maid* (ill. p. 26), or lecherous. Although it is not immediately apparent, the latter vice is presented in Gerard Dou's (1613–1675) *Kitchenmaid Chopping Onions* (1646); this interpretation is justified by the inclusion of onions (an aphrodisiac) and the hanging chicken (traditionally a sign of carnal desire). There is no such lewdness in Vermeer's painting of a kitchen maid. She is taking the business of carefully pouring the thick, curdling milk into a two-handled earthenware bowl very seriously. The maid's eyes are lowered in concentration, and this is a sign of humility and modest introspection.

The bare room ties in well with the simplicity of the maid's way of life and actions. The greyish-yellow wall, with its conspicuous nails (and holes left by ones that have been removed) and cracks – silent testimony of long use – was originally, covered by a map, as has been shown by x-ray examinations of the painting. This would of course have been a symbol of luxury. It is therefore important that Vermeer should have later dispensed with this detail, as it developes the picture of the maid going about her simple everyday duties into something that is almost monumental, despite the small format. She is the embodiment of the "spiritual maid," who was repeatedly extolled in religious treatises.

Caspar Netscher
The Lacemaker, 1662
Oil on canvas, 33 x 27 cm (13 x 10¾ in.)
London, The Wallace Collection

PAGE 64
Detail of *The Lacemaker* (ill. p. 4)

Roemer Visscher
Mignon des Dames
Illustration from *Sinnepoppen*, Amsterdam, 1614, p. 178

The miniature stove filled with glowing coals in Vermeer's *Milkmaid* is a mignon des dames ("favourite of the ladies"). During the coldest months of the year women, when seated, would place these under their voluminous skirts as a welcome source of warmth. In both illustrations and texts of the seventeenth century this source of warmth was often employed as a symbol of female lust, as in the case of a moralizing emblem from the *Sinnepoppen*.

PAGE 67
The Milkmaid, c. 1658–61
Oil on canvas, 45.5 x 41 cm (18 x 16¼ in.)
Amsterdam, Rijksmuseum

This is probably Vermeer's most famous painting. It has been valued highly right from the start, as is shown by the comparatively high price (175 guilders) which this small picture fetched when the paintings in Vermeer's estate were sold in 1696.

Vermeer's contemporaries would certainly have made religious associations with the milk, which the Bible describes as a "sincere" food (1 Peter 2, 2), and likens to "the first principles of the oracles of God" (Hebrews 5, 12). This religious metaphor still echoes in Schiller's phrase, the "milk of devout thought" (*William Tell*, IV, 3). The bread in the basket, and the rolls on the table, are speckled with shimmering points of light and are fascinating examples of Vermeer's wonderful pointillist technique. They, too, have similar religious connotations, given that Christ described himself as the "bread of life" (John 6, 48); it is not possible to miss this reference to the Eucharist.[10]

Books on household management required servants to make a great effort to behave in a god-fearing manner. It was felt that such views were the necessary basis, both for respect of their masters, whom they had to obey, and for an industrious attitude to life.

Vermeer's painting, which is now in New York, of the *Young Woman with a Water Pitcher* (ill. p. 69), is a variation on this theme of virtue, but this time on a higher social scale, that of a middle-class housewife. This woman's eyes are also lowered modestly, and she is evidently pondering over the leaded windows, a motif which appears earlier in the painting *The Girl with the Wineglass* (ill. p. 31). It is not reproduced in any detail in the New York painting, however. What is presented, instead, is an emblematic personification of Temperantia, or temperance, which was considered a cardinal virtue. Hans Burgkmair's (1473–1531) woodcut of a woman pouring water from a jug into a bowl is an example of the traditional way of representing this virtue. And this is the very scene that Vermeer depicts. A young woman is wearing a starched white headcloth and lace trimmings, the transparency of which has been very carefully observed by Vermeer. She is holding the handle of a shining, brightly glistening, gold-coloured jug, which, like the matching bowl, is reflecting the colours of nearby objects.

A similar table set was painted by Robert Campin (c. 1375–1444) on the right wing of the *Werl altar* (1438, Madrid, Museo Nacional del Prado), as part of the symbolism relating to St. Barbara. Like the golden censer and paten, this combination refers to the Holy of Holies in the Jewish Tabernacle. In contrast to this "sacred" object, Vermeer includes the jewellery box of pearls and blue ribbons. This contrast once again embodies conflict, both emotional and material: should this woman be vain and give in to self-love, or should she practise moderation?

Like *The Milkmaid*, Vermeer's *The Lacemaker* (detail p. 64 and ill. p. 4) is also completely absorbed in the concentration and effort required to carry out her work. From the Middle Ages, textiles and needlework had been seen as specifically feminine tasks. In his *Portrait of Anna Codde* (1529, Amsterdam, Rijksmuseum), Maarten van Heemskerck (1498–1574) emphasised spinning flax at a distaff as being a feminine task typical of her. In the Book of Proverbs, the perfect wife is described as being "far above rubies" (31, 11ff.), and as always being busy with wool and with flax, setting her hands to the distaff and the spindle, and making her own quilts and linen sheets. This section of the Old Testament was repeatedly referred to in books on marriage written in and before the seventeenth century.

Vermeer painted this scene in close proximity to his subject. There is one particular feature that suggests that an unfocussed camera obscura was used as an aid in the painting. It is the blurred edges of the colours, in particular of the yellowish-white and red threads, which seem to be streaming from the dark blue

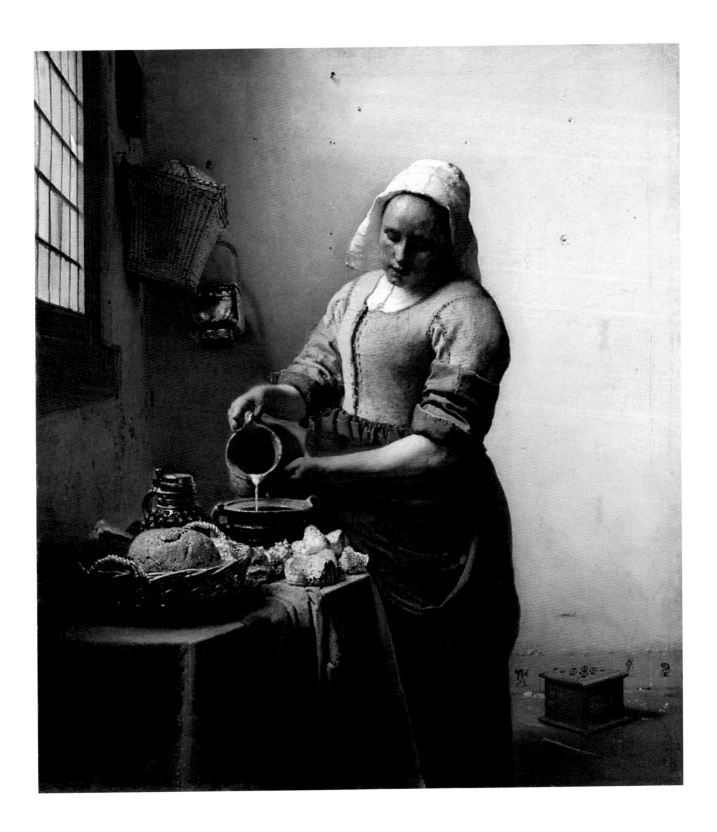

Young Woman with a Water Pitcher, c. 1662–64
Oil on canvas, 45.7 x 40.6 cm (18 x 16 in.)
New York, The Metropolitan Museum of Art,
Gift of Henry G. Marquand, 1889

This woman is torn between conflicting desires:
should she give in to vanity and her wish for
admiration (the box of pearls), or should she
practise moderation (the water pitcher)?

BOTTOM
Detail of *Young Woman with a Water Pitcher*
(ill. p. 69)

The highlights and the reflections in the silver
bowl and the jug are created from small patches,
which when observed at close quarters or
through a magnifying glass evince an almost
abstract pattern. At the same time they convey a
perfect illusion of reality, as shown in the faintly
shimmering colour reflections of the carpet on
the underside of the bowl.

lace pillow with yellow stripes and curling up on the table rug (cf. ill. p. 93).
Vermeer's use of pointillism has an abstract effect on the image, blurring the
other objects used by the woman, such as the lace pillow, the needles around
which she threads the bobbins, and the pattern. This lacemaking equipment is
very conveniently arranged on the wooden stand, quite a contrast to the bare
room in which Caspar Netscher's (c. 1636–1684) *The Lacemaker* (ill. p. 65) is
working, using just a lace pillow.

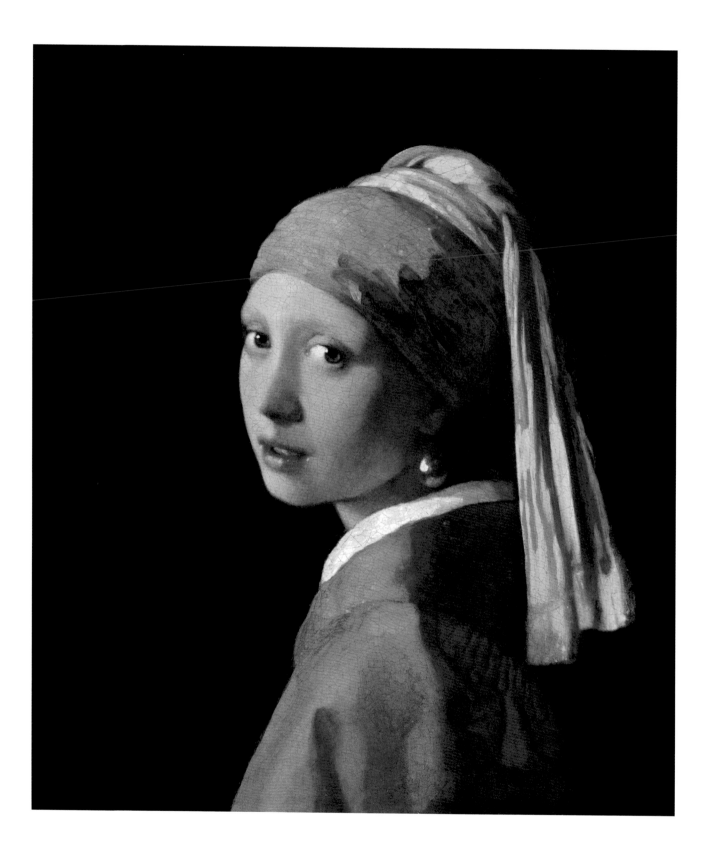

Turbans, Oriental Pearls and Chinoiserie

Portraits of Women

Vermeer predominantly depicted young women in a narrative situation, though this was often merely sketched in. The impression of an activity was created by his addition of some attribute, such as a musical instrument or a set of scales. In addition to these genre-type pictures, however, there are three paintings of his which completely lack any such elements. One cannot help concluding that these must be portraits, especially due to the fact that, in keeping with that genre, we see these women from a close perspective.

One is not forced to accept such a conclusion, of course, because some form of activity or mental action were important attributes in the interpretation of a number of portraits in and before the seventeenth century; and, at the same time, not every picture which appears to be in keeping with the style of a portrait has to be interpreted as a portrait, as having a conscious intention of creating an individualised character. In the case of the portrait historié, for example, where the subject frequently assumed a role in disguise, it is often difficult to decide whether the intention was to portray an individual, or whether the appearance of the model was merely being borrowed for a different purpose.

These considerations are pertinent to Vermeer's famous *Girl with a Pearl Earring* (ill. p. 70), too. The girl is seen against a neutral, dark background, very nearly black, which establishes a powerful three-dimensionality of effect. (In fragment 232 of his *Treatise on Painting*, Leonardo da Vinci had noted that a dark background makes an object appear lighter, and vice versa.) Seen from the side, the girl is turning to gaze at us, and her lips are slightly parted, as if she were about to speak to us. It is an illusionist approach often adopted in Dutch art. She is inclining her head slightly to one side as if lost in thought, yet her gaze is keen.

The girl is dressed in an unadorned, brownish-yellow jacket, and the shining white collar contrasts clearly against it. The blue turban represents a further contrast, while a lemon-yellow, veil-like cloth falls from its peak to her shoulders. Vermeer used plain, pure colours in this painting, limiting the range of tones. As a result, the number of sections of colour are small, and these are given depth and shadow by the use of varnish of the same colour.

The girl's headdress has an exotic effect. Turbans were a popular fashionable accessory in Europe as early as the fifteenth century, as is shown by Jan van

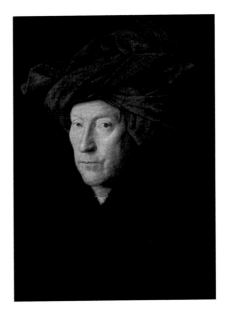

Jan van Eyck
Portrait of a Man (Self-Portrait?), 1433
Oil on oak, 26 x 19 cm (10¼ x 7½ in.)
London, The National Gallery

Turbans were a popular fashion accessory long before they were used by Vermeer, as we see in this probable self-portrait by Jan van Eyck.

PAGE 70
Girl with a Pearl Earring, c. 1665–67
Oil on canvas, 45.5 x 39 cm (18 x 15¼ in.)
The Hague, Koninklijk Kabinet
van Schilderijen Mauritshuis

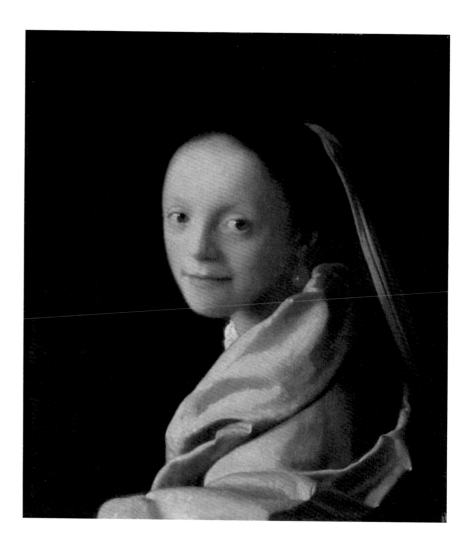

Eyck's (c. 1390–1441) probable self-portrait, now in the National Gallery in London (ill. p. 71). During the wars against the Turks, the remote way of life and foreign dress of the "enemy of Christendom" proved to be very fascinating. A particularly noticeable feature of Vermeer's painting is the large, tear-shaped pearl hanging from the girl's ear; part of it has a golden sheen, and it stands out from the part of the neck which is in shadow.

In his *Introduction to the Devout Life* (1608), which was published in a Dutch translation in 1616, the mystic St. Francis De Sales (1567–1622) wrote, "Both now and in the past it has been customary for women to hang pearls from their ears; as Pliny observed, they gain pleasure from the sensation of the swinging pearls touching them. But I know that God's friend, Isaac, sent earrings to chaste Rebecca as a first token of his love. This leads me to think that this jewel has a spiritual meaning, namely that the first part of the body that a man wants, and which a woman must loyally protect, is the ear; no word or sound should enter it other than the sweet sound of chaste words, which are the oriental pearls of the gospel."[11] From this it is clear that the pearl in Vermeer's painting is a symbol of chastity. The oriental aspect, which is mentioned in the above extract, is further emphasised by the turban. The reference to Isaac and Rebecca suggests that this picture could have been painted on the occasion of this young woman's marriage. So to that extent it is a portrait.

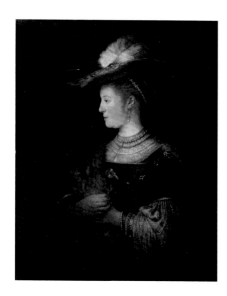

Rembrandt Harmensz. van Rijn
Saskia van Uylenburgh in Sixteenth-Century Costume, 1633/34–42
Oil on board, 99.5 x 78.8 cm (39¼ x 31 in.)
Kassel, Museumslandschaft Hessen Kassel,
Gemäldegalerie Alte Meister

Rembrandt's *Saskia van Uylenburgh* wears a
similar hat as Vermeer's *Girl with the Red
Hat.* Hats of this sort were derived from the
sixteenth-century German *Tellerbarett* (platter
hat), as found in pictures by Lucas Cranach
the Elder.

There is surely a similar explanation for the *Study of a Young Woman* dressed in a smart, grey dress. Many experts on Vermeer have placed this painting (ill. p. 72) among his later ones; since 1979 it has been in The Metropolitan Museum of Art, New York. Though more discreet, there is another pearl earring in this picture. The composition is also related to the other painting. Once again, we see this woman from the side, looking over her shoulder, though her face is turned further towards us. Her black hair is combed back severely from her forehead, and is plaited together with her (bridal?) veil. An additional variant is the position of her left arm, which is bent up against a parapet. Vermeer is following a style of portrait which was introduced by Titian's *Ariosto* (c. 1510, London, National Gallery).

The *Girl with a Flute* (ill. p. 73), which is part of the Widener Collection in Washington, DC, depicts a young girl who is largely detached from the uncertain context of the picture. We see her from a very close angle, leaning on the edge of a table which has been foreshortened to the point where it looks more like a parapet. Again, her lips are lightly parted as she looks at us, as if she were about to speak to us. Her face, and in particular her eyes, are shadowed due to her wide, conical hat; it takes on the appearance of exotic chinoiserie. The way in which her face has been painted in shadow lends a touch of the enigmatic to her features.

Vermeer repeated this posture of the arm in the painting *The Girl with the Red Hat* (ill. p. 75), though she is seen from the other side, and is therefore leaning on her right arm, against the backrest of a chair decorated with lions' heads and rings. This picture was quite evidently painted with the aid of a camera obscura. That is indicated by his use of pointillism, bright dots of paint and occasional highlights on the folds. The light is falling at an angle from above onto her soft, feathery hat; on the top it is vermilion, and the lower shadowed part is a dark purple colour. The intensity of the light is such that the hat appears, at points, to be transparent. Its broad brim has the effect of casting a shadow over most of her face; only her left cheek, below her eye, is lit. The shading of her eyes, the centre of her face, is quite intentional; the principle of *dissimulatio*, a mysterious disguise, is being applied here, the intended effect being to heighten our curiosity.

PAGE 75
The Girl with the Red Hat, c. 1665–67
Oil on board, 22.8 x 18 cm (9 x 7 in.)
Washington, D.C., National Gallery of Art,
Andrew W. Mellon Collection

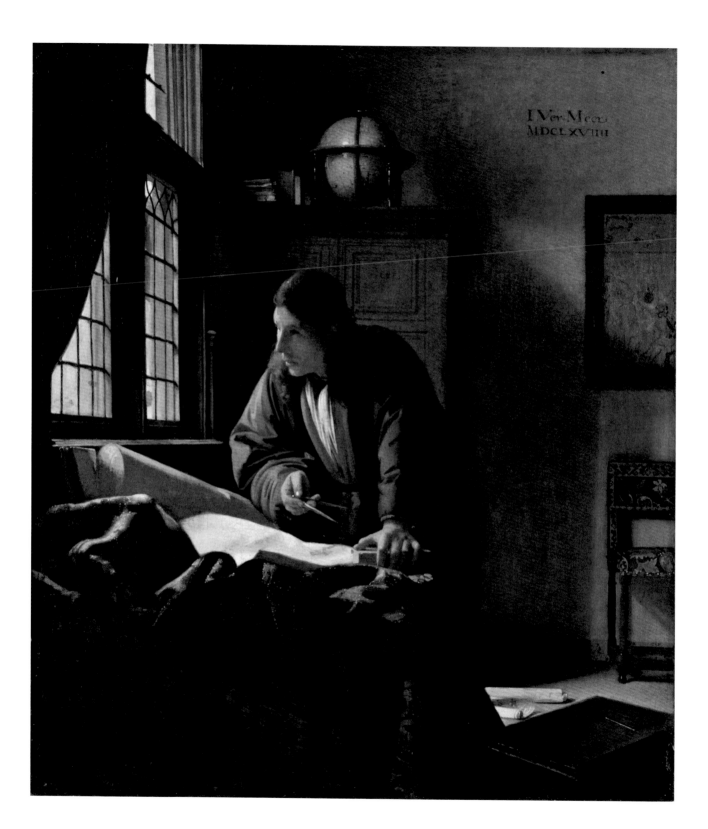

The New Science

Geography and Astronomy

Only three of Vermeer's works can be dated and authenticated precisely; one of them, the 1668 painting *The Astronomer* (ill. p. 78), now hangs in the Louvre. Due to the similar motif and size, it is safe to assume that this painting was conceived as a counterpart to the Frankfurt painting *The Geographer* (ill. p. 76). Both paintings depict an academic, with long hair that is tucked behind his ears, and wearing a robe-like garment that reached to the floor and was not normal everyday attire. This gave these figures an air of mystery, as if they belonged to the chosen few. They are going about their business behind closed doors. The astronomer is not using a telescope, but is at his desk, checking descriptions in an open book against the constellations on his celestial globe. He is using his right hand to hold the globe in a precise position, and we can make out the constellations of the Great Bear (on the left), the Dragon and Hercules (centre), and Lyra (on the right).

James Welu has established that the globe was made by Jodocus Hondius (ill. p. 79), and he has even been able to identify the book. It was written by Adriaen Metius and its title is *Astronomical & Geographical Instructions: Fundamental and Thorough Instructions in Astronomy and Geography by Means of Celestial and Terrestrial Globes* (Amsterdam, 1621).[12] Behind the billowing table carpet it is possible to make out an astrolabe that has been laid down flat; this was an instrument of greatest importance to both astronomy and navigation, as it made it possible to measure angles and ascertain one's position.

The geographer is using compasses to check distances on cartographic plans, the precise details of which cannot be made out. He pauses as he does so, and looks thoughtfully to the window; the light shining through it lights up his face, a sign of inspiration.

Vermeer painted both pictures at a time when a radical change of paradigm was taking place in science. The teachings of conservative humanists such as Sebastian Brant continued up to the middle of the seventeenth century. They taught that it would be presumptuous, and an improper interference in the divine scheme of things, to attempt to discover the nature of the stars and the history, size and composition of the Earth. They imposed a ban on *curiositas*, scientific inquiry, and on any science based on experience and empirical research. In Sebastian Brant's *Ship of Fools*, in the chapter headed "Of the

Jan Verkolje
Portrait of Antoni van Leeuwenhoek, 1680–86
Oil on canvas, 56 x 47.5 cm (22 x 18¾ in.)
Amsterdam, Rijksmuseum

Antoni van Leeuwenhoek (1632–1723) was born in the same year as Vermeer. He was a wealthy cloth merchant, and he experimented with a variety of optical instruments, in particular with the 247 microscopes that he built himself. His discoveries include spermatozoa (1677) and bacteria (1676). He was in close contact with the Royal Society in London, and kept them informed of the results of his research. After Vermeer's death, he was appointed trustee of his estate.

PAGE 76
The Geographer, 1669
Oil on canvas, 51.6 x 45.4 cm (20¼ x 18 in.)
Frankfurt am Main, Städel Museum

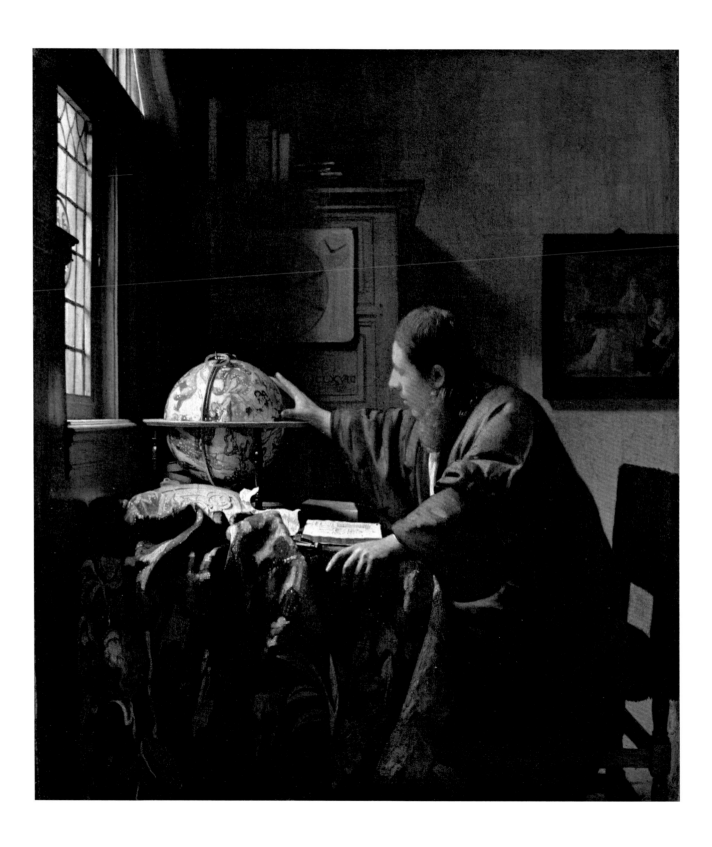

Discovery of all Countries,"[13] it says that classical scientists such as Archimedes and Pliny were careful not to give away their discoveries, or to delve too deeply into the way these were interrelated.

The Astronomer was painted as Louis XIV was building an observatory in Paris (1667–72). In 1668, a young Isaac Newton improved on the design of the reflecting telescope which James Gregory had developed in 1663. A decade previously, Christian Huygens of The Hague had discovered Saturn's sixth satellite with his telescopes. Astronomical activities such as these were of great practical importance for navigation, and in the broadest sense they served (maritime) trade. Such practical considerations and empirical approaches seem to have played little part in Vermeer's astronomer picture. It is typical enough that this astronomer should be working indoors, without looking through the window at the heavens as Gerard Dou's *Astronomer* (1657) does. This suggests that he could be devoting himself to the older, non-empirical science of astrology, or, in other words, that he is drawing up a horoscope. The transition from astrology to astronomy was still in progress at this time. It is known that astronomers such as Johannes Kepler and Tycho Brahe, who were dedicated empiricists, were still practising astrologists. The moment of birth, the stars at nativity, are of key relevance to the forecasting of the future by means of a horoscope; and the concern of Vermeer's painting with this fact is suggested by the picture on the wall, which shows the finding of the infant Moses (Exodus 2, 1–10). The birth of Moses was considered to be a prefiguration of the birth of Christ; Christian teaching therefore perceived a connection between the two, a link grounded in cosmology. The persecution of the children of Israel, including Moses, who was famously left amid the rushes, was compared with the Holy Family's flight to Egypt from Herod's Massacre of the Innocents at Bethlehem.

James Welu, who has inferred the likeliest passage in the work by Adriaen Metius open in front of the astronomer, contends that Metius's accounts of the earliest astronomers were taken by Vermeer to apply to Moses, since the latter (according to Acts 7, 22) was supposedly learned in the wisdom of Egypt, which would have meant astronomy in particular.[14] The question remains, however, why Vermeer should have chosen this specific episode in the story of Moses, which relates in no way to any ability he may have had as an astronomer. As we have seen, Vermeer used this picture of the finding of Moses in a different context (ill. p. 58), in specific allusion to the circumstances of Moses's birth, rather than merely to his person.

Vermeer's *Astronomer* does not make any unambiguous statement on its scientific content. Astrology is not definitely rejected, but neither does the picture argue the case for the new science of astronomy. The geographer is perhaps working more within the terms of our modern understanding of the exact sciences, since the nautical chart on the wall (Willem Jansz. Blaeu's sea chart of Europe, *Pascaarte van alle zee-custen van Europa*, 1600; size of the original 66 x 88 cm), in contrast to the Moses painting, points not to spiritual dimensions but to the practical uses of science in describing the world for the purposes of navigation. In the late 1660s, questions of maritime trade were much on the Dutch nation's mind. Admiral de Ruyter had brought the Second Anglo-Dutch War (1665–67) to a victorious conclusion; this war was fought over supremacy in the North Sea, over fishing rights, and to protect the Dutch merchant fleet, which had been endangered by protective measures that the English government had taken in favour of its own merchants.

Jodocus Hondius
Celestial Globe, 1618

This is the globe which Vermeer included in his painting *The Astronomer*.

PAGE 78
***The Astronomer*, 1668**
Oil on canvas, 51.5 x 45.5 cm (20¼ x 18 in.)
Paris, Musée du Louvre

It has proved possible to identify the book that lies open in front of this mystically-clad astronomer. It was written in 1621 by the astronomer Adriaen Metius. The globe was made by Jodocus Hondius.

"Painted Powerfully and Full of Warmth"

Allegory of Faith

There are two paintings of Vermeer's whose themes differ fundamentally from those of his other, more realistic and everyday pictures. Both have elements of allegory about them, and both set out to realize abstract concepts. One of them portrays a personification of Faith (ill. p. 80); the other shows one of the Muses fitted out with her attributes (ill. p. 85), and she is the key to this painting's meaning.

Herman van Swoll's Amsterdam catalogue, dated 22.4.1699, describes the *Allegory of Faith* as follows: "A sitting Woman with deep meanings, depicting the New Testament [...] powerfully and glowingly painted." The price was set at four hundred guilders, which was a remarkably high figure evidently seeking to do justice to the painter's learned theme, to the painting's size (114.3 x 88.9 cm), and certainly also, as the above comment reveals, to the quality of the painting.

Vermeer studies have long expressed doubt as to whether it is at all correct to identify the theme of this painting as New Testament. A. W. Barnouw demonstrated convincingly in 1914 that Vermeer obviously used Cesare Ripa's *Iconologia* (translated into Dutch by Dirck Pers in 1644); most of the elements employed by Vermeer in his painting appear here as attributes of the allegory of faith, and do not therefore refer to the New Testament. Imprecise or even incorrect identifications of the theme, such as that in the sales catalogue, are more understandable if one takes into account the fact that they were written by amateurs who no longer knew the original intentions of the artist (Vermeer had died twenty-four years before).

Cesare Ripa wrote: "Faith is represented by a sitting woman, who is reverently holding a chalice in her right hand and is resting her left hand on a book which is lying on a solid cornerstone; the latter represents Christ. The world, a globe, lies at her feet. She is dressed in sky blue, with a crimson outer garment. A crushed serpent, and Death, whose arrows have been broken, lie behind the cornerstone. Nearby is an apple, the source of Sin. Behind her, a crown of thorns hangs on a nail (...)" Vermeer did not slavishly follow all these instructions, though it is true that he did keep to most of them. As a result, the red dress, the death motif, and the crown of thorns are all missing, though the latter appears in the painting on the wall, which portrays the crucifixion of Christ as the mystery of faith.

J. C. Jegher
"Capit Quod Non Capit" emblem
Illustration from Guilielmus Hesius,
Emblemata sacra de fide, spe, charitate,
Antwerp, 1636

PAGE 80
Allegory of Faith, c. 1671–74
Oil on canvas, 114.3 x 88.9 cm (45 x 35 in.)
New York, The Metropolitan Museum of Art,
The Friedsam Collection, Bequest of Michael
Friedsam, 1931

Vermeer's *Allegory of Faith* included many of the details in Cesare Ripa's *Iconologia* (1644) and stated how Fides should be represented.

Vermeer probably borrowed the glass ball, which hangs down from the wooden beamed ceiling, from Guilielmus Hesius (*Emblemata sacra de fide, spe, charitate*, Antwerpen, 1636; ill. p. 81), where it was described as a symbol of man's power of reason. This object was originally of prime importance in the art of prophecy, in particular of crystallomancy, divination by means of a crystal ball.

Vermeer moved his scene to the interior of a middle-class home. It is probable that it was one of the larger rooms in the house of his mother-in-law, Maria Thins, whom he and his family lived with; her house provides the setting for many of his genre paintings. The combination of the abstract, bloodless theme of this painting and its everyday "realism" has appeared to many writers on Vermeer to be quite grotesque. Particular points that have given rise to negative judgements are the way Fides is pathetically clutching at her heart, looking skywards (which today seems rather bigoted), and sitting in a complicated posture with her right foot placed on the globe. Arthur Wheelock Jr. said as recently as 1988, "As a work of art it is a failure," and John Nash agrees with this when he says, "It is an odd, unconvincing work."[15]

On the other hand, it must be emphasized that Vermeer's contemporaries judged the painting altogether more positively, as is proved by the high set price. Where the setting is concerned, it should be remembered that this painting is quite in keeping with the tradition of Old Dutch painting (van Dyck and his successors); the application of religious motifs to everyday situations was typical of their work. The purpose of this was to bring the faithful closer to Biblical matters, and to make them experience such as something that closely affected their own lives. Vermeer's *Allegory of Faith* is generally considered to have a Catholic tenor. It has been assumed that the painting was commissioned by the padres of the Delft Jesuit mission, as its symbolism is also related to Jesuit iconography. But there is no firm proof to support this theory.

It is interesting that Vermeer used a globe produced by Hondius in 1618, and it is no accident that its cartouche is turned towards us. Its inscription praises Prince Maurits of Nassau-Orange (1567–1625), who at that time was the Dutch governor. Vermeer was undoubtedly making a political statement by doing this, in the sense that he was demonstrating his allegiance to the House of Orange. Many Delft artists (such as Leonaert Bramer, Christiaen van Couwenbergh and Gerard Houckgeest) shared this attitude, and many of them worked for the Hague court. It is also surely correct to identify the heraldic symbols which adorn the tapestry curtain on the left (a feature Vermeer always used as a motif of revelation) as belonging to the family of this governor. On the one hand there is the orange, on the other a Burgundian lily (top). As descendants of the House of Chalon, members of the House of Orange were titular governors of the Franche-Comté of Burgundy, whose coats of arms included the Fleur de lis.

The Artist's Studio

Vermeer's famous *The Art of Painting* (ill. p. 85), now in Vienna, is seen by many art historians as a programmatic statement, and indeed his testament as an artist. This feeling is expressed by the title which many critics, including Hans Sedlmayr, have given the painting: *In Praise of the Art of Painting*. This adds to the old, and rather more neutral, account in the notary's records, dating from 24 February 1676, when the painting was transferred from Vermeer's widow Catharina Bolnes to her mother, Maria Thins, in order to pay off her debts. There the painting is described as "(...) a picture painted by her aforementioned late husband, depicting the Art of Painting." Once again, as with the *Allegory of*

Detail of *Allegory of Faith* (ill. p. 80)

The glass ball which hangs from the ceiling was borrowed by Vermeer from Guilielmus Hesius's book of emblems (ill. p. 81); it was described there as a symbol of man's power of reason.

Faith, amateurs gave the picture a title which does not properly match its iconographic subject matter. The reason is as follows: the young woman wearing a blue silk robe and yellow skirt and a crown of leaves, holding a trombone in her right hand and a book with a yellow cover in her left, is in no way an allegory of the art of painting (*schilderconst*, Lat. *pictura*); rather – and there is now no doubt about this – she is the Muse Clio, the patron of history.

For a second time, Vermeer was following an outline given in Cesare Ripa's *Iconologia* (in the above-mentioned Dutch edition). The theme of Vermeer's painting is therefore not the art of painting, but history, and in particular the history of famous military victories. This does not of course alter the fact that the painter undoubtedly has a central role in the painting; we see him from behind, anonymous, sitting on a stool in front of his easel, busy painting part of Clio on an otherwise empty canvas. Since the Renaissance, an empty canvas had been a symbol of *concetto*, of artistic inspiration, which takes on palpable shape during the act of painting.

The painter is shown in the process of painting; Vermeer is showing him in a serving role, and therefore this picture cannot be praising the art of painting. The painter is praising not Pictura, but Clio instead, and through her History, or, to be more precise, a particular historical event.

Again the scene is set indoors, perhaps even in Vermeer's own studio, as is suggested by the heavy oak table on the left, which is mentioned in his mother-in-law's inventory. On it are various props which were previously thought to refer to the theory of art. It was assumed that Vermeer was concerned with the problem of the rivalry between the arts, as discussed by Leonardo da Vinci. Painting, understandably enough, was victorious over sculpture, which is symbolised by the mask on the table. The upright book, open folio and silk cloths

Six-Armed Chandelier, c. 1625–50
Brass, height 65 cm, dia. 73 cm /
height 25 ½ in., dia. 28 ¾ in.
Mechelen, Stedelijke Musea

PAGE 85
The Art of Painting, c. 1673
Oil on canvas, 120 x 100 cm (47¼ x 39¼ in.)
Vienna, Kunsthistorisches Museum,
Gemäldegalerie

The woman wearing the crown of leaves, holding a trombone in her right hand and a book in
her left, is Clio, the Muse of History. It is unlike-
ly that Vermeer intended to praise the art of
painting, as has so often been stated; rather, this
allegorical figure appears to be referring to an
actual historical event.

Claes Jansz. Visscher
Wall Map of the Seventeen Provinces, 1636
Coloured engraving, mounted on canvas
Håbo, Skoklosters Slott

can admittedly not be explained within this context. Neither can the relationship
of Clio to these objects. Is the way she is lowering her eyes to be interpreted psy-
chologically as shyness? Is it not, rather, possible that Clio is looking upon the
props as symbols that support her own meaning? If that were the case, they
might well tie in with a particular historical event. But what event could that
have been? A key to this problem could be the map which covers a large part of
the wall. It was produced by Claes Jansz. Visscher (Piscator) in 1636 (ill. p. 84
bottom). It is strange – and this is something that has worried many Vermeer
critics – that he should have chosen to go back to a point of time in Dutch political geography which was long out of date, for the map shows not the region of
the Republic of the northern United Provinces, but – as is also clearly signalled
by the inscription – the seventeen former provinces, as they were before peace
was agreed with Spain in 1609.

The map is bordered on either side by views of cities (on the left, Brussels,
Luxembourg, Ghent, Bergen, Amsterdam, Namur, Leeuwarden, Utrecht,
Zutphen and T'Hof van Hollandt in The Hague; on the right, Limburg,
Nijmegen, Arras, Dordrecht, Middelburg, Antwerp, Mechelen, Deventer,
Groningen and T'Hof van Brabant in Brussels). James Welu has pointed out that
Clio is holding her trombone in front of the view of the Dutch court in The
Hague, which was the residence of the House of Orange (the trombone was a
traditional symbol of gloria, or fame; Clio derives etymologically from the Greek
kléos, or fame).

Vermeer is evidently making a discreet point here. His intention appears to
have been to pay homage to the fame of the House of Orange. But what could
lead him to wish to honour them in this way? One must bear in mind that the
governor, who was a member of the House of Orange, had gradually been losing
his position of authority. In 1653, Jan de Witt (1625–1672), the highest elected of-
ficer of the Staten-Generaal and in receipt of a Council pension, had brought
about the exclusion of the House of Orange from state office under the secret
"Acte van seclusie." The Eternal Edict even withdrew the rank of military com-
mander-in-chief from the young governor, William III (1650–1702). All of this,
which supporters of the governor's party felt to be humiliating, changed at a
stroke when Jan de Witt's regent's party was put on the political defensive due to
the clumsy way it had led the country in the war against France. The only way de
Witt had managed to repel Louis XIV's troops as they invaded the Netherlands
was to open the dykes and flood land. This move, however, caused great damage
to the country's agriculture. Displeasure grew among the population, until at last
he and his brother Cornelis were murdered by an angry mob. This was on 20
August 1672. Now all hopes were pinned on the young governor, William III,
who assumed overall military control and was victorious due to clever tactical
alliances.

Everything points to Vermeer having painted this picture within the historical context of the Franco-Dutch War of 1672–78, and not, as was thought
before, in the mid-1660s. Further support for this hypothesis is the chandelier
with the Habsburg two-headed eagle (ill. p. 84 top); it is no accident that it
is painted just above the top of the map and overlaps with the inscription
OCEANUS GERMANICUS. The term GERMANIA INFERIOR, which was the
old Latin name for the Netherlands, appears to the right. All these are signs of a
positive attitude towards the (Germanic) Holy Roman Empire, and cannot be
coincidences; nor are either the two-headed eagle or the map of the seventeen
provinces familiar features of seventeenth-century Dutch art. They must, there-

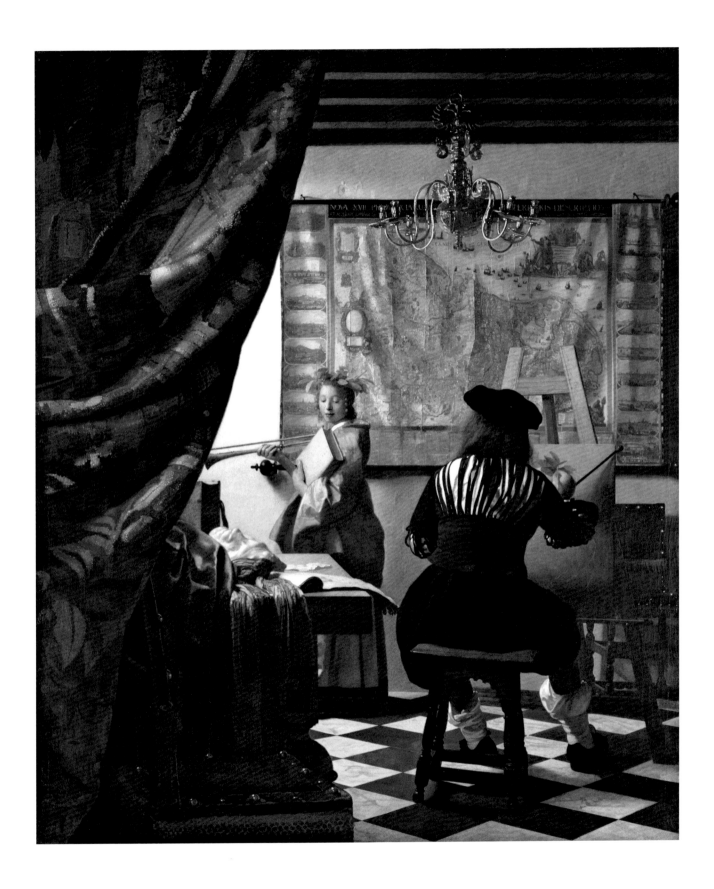

fore, have been included for a particular reason. That reason must have been the alliance which was formed against France on 30 August 1673 by William III and the Habsburg Emperor, Spain and Lorraine. The hopes which were raised by this alliance were sufficient to dispel any remaining aversions which the Dutch may have felt towards the House of Habsburg, whose rule they had fought against a century previously.

Visscher's map, which appears in Vermeer's painting, conjured up memories of the old Burgundian Empire, in which William I of Orange had played an important political role. It should not be forgotten that before he became the leader of the resistance, forced into that position more by circumstances than political conviction, he was a favourite of Charles V, who made him Governor of Holland, Zeeland, Utrecht and the Burgundian Franche-Comté. The Franche-Comté was the most fiercely fought-over area during the Franco-Dutch War; Louis XIV did not conquer it until spring 1674. This aspect is alluded to by Vermeer's clothing his painter in Burgundian dress of the early sixteenth century. Since Clio, as Muse of History, draws a veil of glory over military success, the painting was presumably intended to convey confidence of victory; it can only have been painted before the loss of the Franche-Comté, in other words at a time when the Dutch still hoped to save it from conquest. This points to a date in the last third of 1673.

The props on the table are presumably Vermeer's way of alluding to William I, who united all the Dutch provinces in the Ghent Concorde of 1576. It is possible that Vermeer is also referring to the magnificent tomb of the House of Orange in the Delft Nieuwe Kerk, which was created by Hendrick de Keyser (1623). There, too, a fama holding a trombone appears, at the feet of the marble statue of William on the tomb. The mask lying on the table in the painting, which has noticeably individualised features, could be based on the head of the figure on the tomb, or on a terracotta mask of William I by Hendrick de Keyser which is in the Prinsenhof in Delft.

Older interpretations of this painting were based on a twentieth-century understanding of art, and considered the picture to be in praise of the art of painting, or a glorification of the profession of painting; in contrast to these, what should be emphasised more strongly is its political meaning, Vermeer making a statement on the historical events of the day.

PAGE 87
Detail of *The Art of Painting* (ill. p. 85)

The Rediscovery of Vermeer

Vermeer and the Impressionists

Despite what has often been said in the past, Johannes Vermeer van Delft was never completely forgotten. He is mentioned with praise in the seventeenth and eighteenth centuries; compared with other contemporary artists, though, this opinion met with little response.

It is only since the middle of the nineteenth century that his art has enjoyed an increasingly enthusiastic reception. It is no coincidence that this dawning interest in Vermeer went hand in hand with the rise of Impressionism, whose agenda was the rejection of a dark-toned, academic style of painting in favour of brightly-lit plein-air painting using a full, unmixed palette. It was the French socialist politician and journalist Théophile Thoré-Bürger (1807–1869) who initiated the new appreciation of Vermeer's art.

During his travels through England, Belgium, Holland and Switzerland, Thoré-Bürger concerned himself intensively with Dutch seventeenth-century painting and its everyday realism. He found that it corresponded to the aesthetic ideas expressed in the theories of Jules Champfleury (1821–1889) and Pierre-Joseph Proudhon (1809–1865), and in the art of the Barbizon school and Gustave Courbet (1819–1877).

A major plank in the French realist platform was that present-day social, cultural and political subject matter should determine content. This position was adopted by the Impressionists, though they aimed for radical change in terms of technique as well.

For the Impressionists, colour was a function of the response to light. Its brightness, tonality and density were dependent on the wavelength of light (or ethereal vibrations, as contemporary terminology had it). The Impressionists drew upon scientific theory, with the result that colour was seen no longer as intrinsic to things, but rather as a phenomenon subject to changes in the light. Furthermore, it was also particularly dependent on processes of perception in the eye of the beholder.

It was this theory of colour as a phenomenon of light that sensitized Thoré-Bürger's eye for what was aethetically distinctive in Vermeer: "In Vermeer, the light is never artificial; it is precise and natural, and not even a meticulous physicist could wish it to be more exact (...)." Elsewhere, he wrote: "It is to this precision of light that Vermeer owes the harmony of his colours too." One might say

"How shall I describe these portraits by Rembrandt and Hals, and this view of Delft by Vermeer, these masterpieces which come so close to Impressionism?"

— CAMILLE PISSARRO, 1882

PAGE 88
Detail of *The Milkmaid* (ill. p. 67)

The allconquering illusionism in Vermeer's rendering of the surfaces of objects is owed to the velvety lustre of paint applied in minute dots, a technique already termed *pointillé* by Theophile Thoré-Bürger, who drew attention to it as one of the characteristic marks of any work by Vermeer.

Detail of *A Lady Writing a Letter with Her Maid* (ill. p. 58)

The picture is dominated by long, unbroken contours and straight lines, which create large forms: the heavy green curtain in the dark left foreground that hangs almost vertically, the parallel folds of the white curtain at the window and the narrow strip of wall beside it.

that Thoré-Bürger was discovering "modern" qualities in Vermeer, qualities in his artistic approach that had gone beyond the scope of the reception in his own day, but offered an ample purchase for appreciation two centuries later.

We now know that Vermeer used a camera obscura (ill. p. 16) for most of his paintings. What is more, far from hiding the effects of the instrument, such as unfocussed outlines and the famous pointillist dots of light, he drew attention to them (cf. ill. p. 88). This lends his paintings an "abstract" quality, since they do not pretend to be reproducing reality as it is, but show it as it is seen. In terms of Vermeer's work method, this translates as using a medium of reproduction to grasp the thing perceived – at a remove. We might even say that the camera obscura became a source of his style.

This hidden tendency to abstraction in Vermeer's technique was the cornerstone of his growing fame in the last third of the nineteenth century. Today, he is generally seen with Rembrandt and Frans Hals (1580/85–1666) – the latter being another kindred spirit of the Impressionists – as the third great Dutch artist of the Golden Age.

Vincent van Gogh (1853–1890) gave very close attention to Eugène Delacroix' theory of colour, and, like the Neo-Impressionists, studied the problems of complementary and contrasting colours in considerable detail. In a letter to Emile Bernard, written somewhere around 1888, he waxed lyrical on the subject of Vermeer's colour harmonies: "This strange painter's palette is blue, lemon yellow, pearl grey, black, white (...) the arrangement (...) is as characteristic of him as the black, white, grey, pink is of Velázquez." In 1883, the French art historian Henri Havard observed that many of the figures in Vermeer's paintings seemed merely to be "happy dabs of paint," commenting: "If they have any important part in the harmonic symphony at all, it is due to the shape they make, rather than the thought they express."

This new admiration for Vermeer is evident not only in the visual arts but also in classic Modernist literature. The most famous example is surely Marcel Proust's eulogy in *A la recherche du temps perdu* (1923), in Part V, *La prisonnière*, where the death of Bergotte the writer is described. Shortly before, a critic has told the writer that he will be able to see Vermeer's *View of Delft* (ill. pp. 16/17), on loan from the Mauritshuis in The Hague for an exhibition. "At last he stood before the Vermeer, which in his memory was more radiant, even more different from anything else he was familiar with, but in which, thanks to the critic's article, he made out for the first time little blue-clothed figures, and furthermore realised that the sand was tinted a rosy colour, and finally discovered the costly material of the tiny yellow wall as well. His dizziness grew; he fixed his gaze – as a child would on a yellow butterfly it wants to catch – on that costly little corner of wall. 'That is how I should have written,' he reflected. 'My last books are too dry, I should have used more colour, should have made my language as precious in itself as this little yellow corner of wall is' (...)" For the writer nearing death, that detail becomes the very definition of art: "(...) this yellow corner of wall, done with such great skill and exquisite subtlety by a painter who remains unknown for all time and is only identified for convenience by the name Vermeer."

One could continue the list of quotations. Artists and theorists of nearly all avant-garde types of art have praised Vermeer's feeling for real colour and his principle of avoiding all unnecessary detail in his compositions. Paul Cézanne's (1839–1906) insistence that the artist should resist the literary became programmatic for avant-garde artists concerned primarily with questions of form; and it was little wonder, given this view, that Vermeer was felt to be free of anecdotal, narrative elements. André Malraux (1901–1976) in particular emphasised that Vermeer's work completely lacked the "myth of narrative action" and "for the first time in the history of art (…) the subject of the painting had become an object of vision."[16]

The aesthetics of art as a mirror of culture

Those who have rediscovered Vermeer since the late nineteenth century have recognised that he was quietly innovative in his compositional technique. His predilection for balance; his method of simplifying complex structures to a few components (a method in which geometry played a key role); his treatment of light, which achieved effects of an almost plein-airist nature, rendering shadows no longer in greys but in a shimmer of colour; and his very paintwork, so distinctively different from the fine, porcelain-smooth application then usual in the Netherlands – all of these characteristics were the hallmarks of a style unusual even in Vermeer's own day.

If we describe his work only in these terms, though, we risk missing how very concrete Vermeer's representational art is. His subjects are by no means of secondary importance. On closer inspection, we realise in fact that the formal features of Vermeer's style derive from his way of placing people, objects and rooms in contexts that lend social and cultural meaning. It is of the essence that his strongly individualized figures tend to appear alone or almost alone, busy at everyday tasks, reading letters or pouring milk. There is no bustle, tension or agitation of the kind typical of Dutch narrative genre paintings of the period. The facial expressions of Vermeer's people are not distorted grimaces dictated by affect. His figures, mainly women, seem almost free of passion, not in any sense of being emotionally unresponsive or insensible but in a sense of masking their feelings rather than thrusting them upon us.

In his age, Vermeer was almost unrivalled in his ability to address by visual means the moral agenda drawn up by thinkers such as Gracián or Montaigne. He too was concerned to define people in their individuality, to preserve a private domain for the affairs of the spirit, and to place limits upon communication. It might not be going too far to see the tables that so often appear in the foregrounds of his interiors, with carpets or curtains draped across them, as symbolic: though it is only a prop, the table nonetheless denotes a boundary, and imposes distance between ourselves and the private realm we are permitted to see.

Rhetoric is of diminished importance in Vermeer, though it does not altogether disappear. Rather, it is frequently transformed into a barely perceptible irony, as becomes clear if we consider the interplay between the central characters and visual quotations, so important for the overall meaning. In many of Vermeer's paintings there are pictures on the walls, pictures clearly related to the protagonists and intended by the artist as *clavis interpretandi*, or aids to interpretation. His conception of the visual image was evidently dialectic: while he may at first glance seem indifferent to communicating the meaning of a painting, he does in fact supply discreet aids such as we can only make use of if we have the necessary learning and can pick up allusions.

Vermeer was frequently inspired by sayings and moral adages, such as circulated in large quantities in the illustrated emblem books of the time. In the sixteenth century, when they first appeared, emblems were originally symbols devised by humanists to suggest mysterious deeper meanings in things, and were difficult to interpret; but by the seventeenth century they had undergone lasting change. In the Netherlands they had become more accessible, and had taken on an unmistakable function as a source of popular education. They were meant to establish and consolidate a new moral code, and to shape and regulate individual conduct within emerging middle class society.

In the early modern era, the family unit was of central importance. Much of society's vital work was done in the family. Since the increasing division of labour was now tending to involve many men in work outside the home, women, as keepers of the house, found themselves with greater responsibility to bear and more tasks to perform. And the powers that were, as well as the authors of popular didactic tracts, tirelessly reminded them of these.

Most of Vermeer's paintings are about these domestic duties, but they also show the conflicts called forth in women by the imperatives of duty and virtue, so much at odds with the libidinous desires they were no longer permitted to express. We may be tempted to see Vermeer's method of encoding his meanings, and the concomitant impression of reserve and discretion his characters make, in purely aesthetic terms. But in fact they may be a response to this process of socio-cultural change. Arguably Vermeer's figures, rejecting the norms and demands of society, have been forced into isolation, and have withdrawn modestly – into silence.

PAGE 93
Detail of *The Lacemaker* (ill. p. 4)

Especially impressive in the picture *The Lacemaker* are the abstract foreground forms made up of colour spots, used by Vermeer to evoke the white and red threads spilling out of the sewing cushion on to a table carpet. It is only upon closer inspection that this tangle of colour and forms can be made out for what it is.

Johannes Vermeer
1632–1675
Life and Work

1615 Reynier Janszoon Vos, by occupation a silk worker, marries Digna (or Dymphna) Baltens in Amsterdam. They then settle in Delft, where Reynier later (in 1641) purchases and runs the "Mechelen," an inn on the Market Square.

1622 Carel Fabritius (1622–1654) is born in Midden-Beemster.

1626 Jan Steen (1626–1679) is born in Leiden.

1631 Reynier Janszoon Vos starts dealing in paintings, and is enrolled in the Delft artists' guild, the Guild of St. Luke.

1632 Johannes Vermeer, the second child of Reynier Janszoon Vos and Digna Baltens, is born. Their first child was a daughter. Antonie van Leeuwenhoek (1632–1723) is born in Delft.

1648 The Thirty Years' War comes to an end with the Treaty of Westphalia.

1650 William III of Orange is born.

1652 Vermeer's father dies. Carel Fabritius is made a member of the Guild of St. Luke.

1652–54 First Anglo-Dutch naval war.

1653 Vermeer marries Catharina Bolnes, the daughter of Maria Thins. The marriage is witnessed by the painter Leonaert Bramer (1596–1674). On 29 December, Vermeer is admitted as a Master Painter to the Guild of St. Luke.

1654 The Delft magazine explodes on 12 October, killing the painter Carel Fabritius.

1656 First dated work of Vermeer's (*The Procuress*, Dresden, Gemäldegalerie Alte Meister).

1657 Vermeer borrows two hundred guilders.

1662 Vermeer is elected as syndic (hooftman) of the Guild of St. Luke.

1663 The French nobleman Balthazar de Monconys, an alchemist and lover of art, visits Vermeer and writes about this encounter in his Journal.

1665–67 Second Anglo-Dutch naval war.

1667 The Spanish Netherlands are occupied by Louis XIV. In response, the Netherlands form a triple alliance with England and Sweden, thereby forcing Louis XIV largely to abandon his conquests. Dirck van Bleyswijck mentions Vermeer in his *Beschrijvinge der Staat Delft* (*Description of Delft*).

1668 Second dated work of Vermeer's (*The Astronomer*, Paris, Musée du Louvre).

1669 Third dated work of Vermeer's (*The Geographer*, Frankfurt am Main, Städel Museum).

1670–71 Vermeer is re-elected as syndic of the Guild.

1670 Vermeer's mother dies, leaving him his parents' inn, the "Mechelen."

1672 Louis XIV invades the Netherlands from the Lower Rhine with an army of 100,000 men. The only way the Netherlands can defend themselves against the advancing troops is to open the dykes and flood land. Vermeer lets the "Mechelen" for 180 guilders a year. He also journeys to The Hague, where, together with Johannes Jordaens, he is employed by the Elector of Brandenburg to value Italian paintings.

1675 Vermeer travels to Amsterdam to borrow one hundred guilders. He dies on 13 or 14 December, and is buried in the Oude Kerk in Delft on 15 December. He is survived by eleven under-age children, eight of whom are still living at home. He is deeply in debt at the time of his death, and as a result his widow has no alternative but to be declared bankrupt. Delft city records show that Van Leeuwenhoek is appointed as curator of his estate on 30 September 1676.

1688 Vermeer's widow, Catharina Bolnes, dies.

Notes

1 Biography of Vermeer: Cf. research by J. M. Montias, *Vermeer and his Milieu*, Princeton, 1989.

2 Prices of paintings: J. M. Montias, *Artists and Artisans in Delft*, Princeton, 1982, pp. 196f, and P. C. Sutton, in: cat. *Masters of 17th Century Dutch Landscape Painting*, Amsterdam, 1987.

3 Cf. J. Nash: *Vermeer*, London, 1991, p. 46.

4 Cf. Jan Baptista van Helmont's (1577–1644) medical treatises *Ortus medicinae* (Amsterdam, 1648; 2, 1652) and *Opuscula medica inaudita* (Cologne, 1648).

5 Cat. *Sprache der Bilder*, Brunswick, 1978, p. 117.

6 Is this woman really pregnant, as is suggested repeatedly in books on Vermeer? It is possible that what she is wearing is a crinoline farthingale. These bell-shaped skirts were in fashion at the time, as is confirmed in a 1641 painting by Johannes Verspronck, which features a girl wearing such a dress (Amsterdam, Rijksmuseum). Farthingales were called "vertugalles" or "vertugadins" (chastity skirts).

7 Cf. A. Henkel/A. Schöne (eds.): *Emblemata*, Stuttgart, 1967, col. 1292.

8 P. Chaunu: *Europäische Kultur im Zeitalter des Barock*, Munich/Zurich, 1968, p. 259. Also cf. J.-L. Flandrin: *Familien. Sozologie – Ökonomie – Sexualität*, Frankfurt/M., 1978.

9 Cf. an important source: Peter Müller: *Dissertatio Juridica de litteris amatoriis quam praeside Petro Müllero (...) 1679 publicè ventilandam exhibet Bernhard Pfretzschner*, Gera/Jena, 1690 (makes frequent references to writings on marriage, e.g. J. L. Vives, D. Covarrubias y Leyva, and also to emblems whose significance has been clearly established).

10 Servants inseventeenth-century households were divided according to their duties and positions. In contrast to cowmaids, who worked in the stables and outside the house, the milkmaid's tasks lay within the house. She had to manage the rather complex dairy. Her duties included producing curds, butter and cheese, cleaning all the necessary utensils, such as the milk churns and muslin cloths, and keeping the dairy clear of vermin (one way of doing this was to fumigate it with myrrh, incense and various herbs). Given the importance of milk products, it is

not surprising that milk took on an almost religious importance.

11 Cf. E. de Jongh: "Pearls of virtue and pearls of vice," in: *Simiolus* 8, 1875/76, , p. 77.
12 Cf. J. A. Welu: "Vermeer: His Cartographic Sources," in: *The Art Bulletin* LVII, 1975, pp. 529–47.
13 Sebastian Brant: *Das Narrenschiff*, ed. by C. Traeger, Frankfurt/M., 1980, ill. 187ff.
14 Cf. J. A. Welu: "Vermeer's Astronomer: Observations on an open book," in: *The Art Bulletin* LXVIII, No. 2, June 1986, pp. 263–67.
15 Cf. A. Wheelock jr.: *Jan Vermeer*, New York, 1988, ill. p. 118; Nash (see note 3), p. 108.
16 The quotations from Thoré-Bürger, Havard and Malraux are taken from: G. Aillaud et al. , *Vermeer*, Geneva, 1987, ill. pp. 209 ff. (Acknowledgements), and I. Schlégl/ILL. P. Bianconi: *Das Gesamtwerk von Vermeer*, Luzern/Freudenstadt/Vienna, 1967, pp. 10ff. The quotations from Proust are taken from: *A la recherche du temps perdu*, Vol. V: *La Prisonnière*. Cf. also Yann le Pichon (in colaboration with Anne Borrel): *Le musée retrouvé de Marcel Proust*, Paris, 1990. pp. 84–86. – On Thoré-Bürger cf. A Blankert: *Vermeer of Delft*, Oxford, 1978, pp. 67ff. On the camera obscura as the "source of style" cf. S. Alpers: *Kunst als Beschreibung*, Cologne, 1985, p. 87.

Picture credits

The publisher wishes to thank the museums, private collections, archives and photographers who granted permission to reproduce works and gave support in the making of the book. Where not otherwise indicated, the reproductions were based on material in the publisher's archive. In addition to the collections and museums named in the picture captions, we wish to credit the following:

Agenzia Fotografica Scala, Antella, Florence: pp. 22 bottom, 78
bpk | Gemäldegalerie | SMB, Berlin: pp. 20 top, 62 (Jörg P. Anders), 34/35, 59, 63 (Volker Schneider)
bpk | The Metropolitan Museum of Art, New York: pp. 24, 27, 33 bottom left, 33 bottom right, 45, 68, 69, 72, 80, 83
bpk | Staatliche Kunstsammlungen Dresden (Herbert Boswank): pp. 23, 48, 51
© Bridgeman Art Library, Berlin/London: pp. 30, 40
© The Frick Collection, New York: pp. 32, 38/39, 55
Herzog Anton Ulrich-Museum, Brunswick, Kunstmuseum des Landes Niedersachsen (Claus Cordes): pp. 28, 31
© Koninklijk Kabinet van Schilderijen Mauritshuis, The Hague: pp. 21, 49, 70
Koninklijke Bibliotheek, The Hague: pp. 36, 81

Kunsthistorisches Museum, Vienna: pp. 2, 33 top left, 85, 87
© Musée du Louvre, Dist. RMN-Grand Palais, Paris (Georges Poncet): p. 25
Museumslandschaft Hessen, Kassel: p. 74
© National Galleries of Scotland, Edinburgh: p. 18
© National Gallery, London: pp. 13, 26, 37, 42, 43, 46, 71
© National Gallery of Art, Washington: pp. 14, 54, 56/57, 61, 73, 75
© National Gallery of Ireland, Dublin: pp. 58, 90
Österreichische Nationalbibliothek, Vienna: p. 16
Rijksmuseum, Amsterdam: pp. 6, 9, 12, 15, 33 top right, 50, 52, 60, 67, 88
© Photo RMN-Grand Palais, Paris: pp. 4, 64, 93 (Gérard Blot), 19 (René-Gabriel Ojéda)
Gordon H. Robertson: p. 47
The Royal Collection © 2009, Her Majesty Queen Elizabeth II, London: pp. 29, 47
© Städel Museum (U. Edelmann), Frankfurt a. M. – Artothek, Weilheim: pp. 76, 94
Stedelijke Musea, Mechelen: p. 84 top
© Margareta Svensson, Amsterdam: pp. 11, 16/17

Imprint

EACH AND EVERY TASCHEN BOOK PLANTS A SEED!
TASCHEN is a carbon neutral publisher. Each year, we offset our annual carbon emissions with carbon credits at the Instituto Terra, a reforestation program in Minas Gerais, Brazil, founded by Lélia and Sebastião Salgado. To find out more about this ecological partnership, please check: *www.taschen.com/zerocarbon*
Inspiration: unlimited. Carbon footprint: zero.

To stay informed about TASCHEN and our upcoming titles, please subscribe to our free magazine at *www.taschen.com/magazine*, follow us on Twitter, Instagram, and Facebook, or e-mail your questions to *contact@taschen.com*.

© 2016 TASCHEN GmbH
Hohenzollernring 53, D–50672 Köln
www.taschen.com

Original edition:
© 1993 Benedikt Taschen Verlag GmbH

Editing by Norbert Schneider and Burkhard Riemschneider, Cologne
Translation by Fiona Hulde, Newcastle-under-Lyme
Design by Birgit Eichwede, Cologne
Production by Tina Ciborowius, Cologne

Printed in Slovakia
ISBN 978–3–8365–0489–8

PAGE 2
The Art of Painting (detail), c. 1673
Oil on canvas, 120 x 100 cm (47¼ x 39¼ in.)
Vienna, Kunsthistorisches Museum, Gemäldegalerie

PAGE 4
The Lacemaker, c. 1669/70
Oil on canvas, mounted on board, 23.9 x 20.5 cm (9½ x 8 in.)
Paris, Musée du Louvre